Bulletin
of the European Union

Supplement 15/97

Commission opinion on Slovenia's application for membership of the European Union

Document drawn up on the basis of COM(97) 2010 final

European Commission

ZZ
EM115
97B15

C

A great deal of additional information on the European Union is available on the Internet.
It can be accessed through the Europa server (http://europa.eu.int)

Cataloguing data can be found at the end of this publication

Luxembourg: Office for Official Publications of the European Communities, 1997

ISBN 92-828-1237-5

Printed in Belgium

PRINTED ON CHLORINE-FREE BLEACHED PAPER

Contents

A — Introduction

a) Preface

Application for Membership

Slovenia presented its application for membership of the European Union on 10 June 1996, and the Council of Ministers decided on 15 July 1996 to implement the procedure laid down in Article O of the Treaty, which provides for consultation of the Commission.

That is the framework in which the Commission submits the present Opinion, responding to the request of the European Council in Madrid in December 1995 to present the Opinion as soon as possible after the conclusion of the Intergovernmental Conference, which commenced in March 1996 and concluded in June 1997.

Context of the Opinion

The Slovenian application for membership is being examined at the same time as applications from nine other associated countries. Slovenia's accession is to be seen as part of an historic process, in which the countries of Central and Eastern Europe overcome the division of the continent which has lasted for more than 40 years, and join the area of peace, stability and prosperity created by the Union.

The European Council in Copenhagen in June 1993 concluded that:

'The associated countries in Central and Eastern Europe that so desire shall become members of the Union. Accession will take place as soon as a country is able to assume the obligations of membership by satisfying the economic and political conditions.

Membership requires:

☐ that the candidate country has achieved stability of institutions guaranteeing democracy, the rule of law, human rights and respect for and protection of minorities;

☐ the existence of a functioning market economy, as well as the capacity to cope with competitive pressure and market forces within the Union;

☐ the ability to take on the obligations of membership, including adherence to the aims of political, economic and monetary union.

The Union's capacity to absorb new members, while maintaining the momentum of European integration, is also an important consideration in the general interest of both the Union and the candidate countries'.

This declaration spelled out the political and economic criteria for examining the accession requests of the associated countries of Central and Eastern Europe.

The European Council in Madrid in December 1995 referred to the need, in the context of the pre-accession strategy, 'to create the conditions for the gradual, harmonious integration of the application countries, particularly through:

☐ the development of the market economy,

☐ the adjustment of their administrative structure,

☐ the creation of a stable economic and monetary environment'.

In its Opinion, the Commission analyses the Slovenian application on its merits, but according to the same criteria as the other applications, on which it is delivering Opinions at the same time. This way of proceeding respects the wish, expressed by the European Council in Madrid, to ensure that the applicant countries are treated on an equal basis.

In addition to the individual Opinions the Commission is presenting separately to the Council, in the framework of its communication 'Agenda 2000', a general assessment of the accession requests, and its recommendations concerning the strategy for successful enlargement of the Union. At the same time, it is presenting an evaluation of the impact of enlargement on the Union's policies.

Contents of the Opinion

The structure of the Opinion takes account of the conclusions of the European Council in Copenhagen. It:

☐ describes the relations up to now between Slovenia and the Union, particularly in the framework of the association agreement;

☐ analyses the situation in respect of the political conditions mentioned by the European Council (democracy, rule of law, human rights, protection of minorities);

☐ assesses Slovenia's situation and prospects in respect of the economic conditions mentioned by the European Council (market economy, capacity to cope with competitive pressure);

☐ addresses the question of Slovenia's capacity to adopt the obligations of membership, that is the *acquis* of the Union as expressed in the Treaty, the secondary legislation, and the policies of the Union;

☐ makes finally a general evaluation of Slovenia's situation and prospects in respect of the conditions for membership of the Union, and a recommendation concerning accession negotiations.

In assessing Slovenia in respect of the economic criteria and its capacity to assume the *acquis*, the Commission has included a prospective assessment; it has attempted to evaluate the progress which can reasonably be expected on the part of Slovenia in the coming years, before accession, taking account of the fact that the *acquis* itself will continue to develop. For this purpose, and without prejudging the actual date of accession, the Opinion is based on a medium-term time horizon of approximately five years.

During the preparation of the Opinion, the Commission has obtained a wealth of information on Slovenia's situation from the Slovenian authorities, and has utilised many other sources of information, including the Member States and numerous international organisations.

b) Relations between the European Union and Slovenia

Historical and Geopolitical Context

Slovenia lies on the Adriatic Sea in the triangle between Central, Southern and Southeast Europe, bordering four countries (Italy, Austria, Hungary and Croatia). Its area is 20 250 km^2 and its population 2 million.

The territory of Slovenia has been largely settled by Slav populations since the 6th century. In the 13th century power passed into the hands of the Habsburg dynasty. Following the First World War and the collapse of the Austro-Hungarian Empire, Slovenia opted to become part of the Kingdom of Serbs, Croatians and Slovenes (later Yugoslavs). During the Second World War, Slovenia was occupied by both Germany and Italy.

In 1945 Slovenia became part of the Socialist Federal Republic of Yugoslavia, though the coast and hinterland remained under international administration until 1954. After a period of orthodox communist policies of expropriation and collectivisation, the Constitutional Law of 1953 established the foundations of Yugoslav self-management socialism. The 1963 Constitution fostered the notion of a self-managed society at all levels of economic, social and cultural life, which remained however largely controlled by the Communist Party.

A weakening of federal authority and the devolution of powers to the republics began in the late sixties, but authoritarian centralism returned after political disturbances in 1972. Following the death of Tito in May 1980 political and economic disintegration gained momentum. Accelerating inflation, growing balance of payment deficits and rapid increases in borrowing added impetus to requests for regional autonomy and the introduction of parliamentary democracy. In 1989, fearing Serbian domination, the Slovene Assembly amended the Constitution to pave the way for a sovereign Slovenian State.

The first free elections in Slovenia were carried in April 1990. In a referendum on 23 December 1990, 88 % of the votes favoured independence.

The 'Basic Constitutional Charter on Independence and Sovereignty of Slovenia' was adopted on 25 June 1991 and independence proclaimed the day after. Victory in the 10-day war against the Yugoslav National Army following the independence proclamation confirmed Slovenia's status as an independent state. Slovenia was recognised on 15 January 1992 by the European Community. Presidential and legislative elections in December 1992 led to the formation of a broad coalition government. New legislative elections in 1996 were followed by several months in which no group of parties could establish a working majority.

Slovenia's Position concerning the European Union

Since independence the Slovene Government has consistently underlined its foreign policy priority of integration with the European Union. As early as February 1992 it sought a Europe Agreement and support for the restructuring and consolidation of the Slovene economy.

As soon as the Cooperation Agreement with the EU entered into force in 1993, the Slovenian Government sought the opening of negotiations for a Europe Agreement. On 10 June 1996, the day the Europe Agreement was signed, the Government formally requested EU membership. Two months earlier the Assembly adopted a declaration restating this as its objective and noting its willingness to liberalise the real estate market on the basis of the principles set out at the Madrid European Council. In May 1997 Slovenia issued a document on its EU accession strategy, reconfirming its ambition to become a full member of the EU and that she is 'not only able and willing to assume the obligations deriving from full membership but also ready to accept certain limitations which the realisation of these obligations would bring for the sovereignty of the Slovene State.'

Contractual Relations

The Socialist Federal Republic of Yugoslavia reached a series of trade agreements with the EC, the first dating from 1970. In 1980 a Trade and Economic Cooperation Agreement, the first of its kind, was signed, accompanied by the establishment of a Cooperation Council. Even then,

96% of Yugoslav industrial products exported to the EU were tax exempt, while 28% of agricultural products benefited from preferential treatment. Following the outbreak of civil war in Yugoslavia, the EC suspended this Agreement in November 1991. Since then, annually renewed autonomous preferential trade regimes have provided for continuity in trade relations, until the entry into force of an Interim Agreement in January 1997 (see below).

Diplomatic relations between the EU and Slovenia were established on 13 April 1992. On 1 September 1993 a Cooperation Agreement, essentially modelled on the one signed in 1980 with Yugoslavia, accompanied by supplementary arrangements in particular on transport, textile and financial cooperation, entered into force.

After one meeting in 1993, the political dialogue envisaged under this Agreement was never pursued, because of the expectation that it would soon be overtaken by a Europe Agreement. Conclusion of this was, however, delayed by differences over the need for amendments to Slovene real estate legislation to permit EU nationals to own property. An exchange of letters annexed to the Europe Agreement finally paved the way for its signature on 10 June 1996. According to these the Slovene real estate market would be opened to all EU citizens four years after entry into force of the Europe Agreement, but would be already liberalised on entry into force for those EU citizens who have lived for at least three years on the territory of Slovenia.

Pending ratification of the Europe Agreement, an Interim Agreement entered into force on 1 January 1997 which covers all trade and trade-related fields under the Europe Agreement and in these fields replaces the Cooperation Agreement and the annual autonomous trade measures. Economic cooperation under the Cooperation Agreement will continue.

Once it enters into force, the Europe Agreement will be the legal basis for relations between Slovenia and the Union. Its aim is to provide a framework for political dialogue, promote the expansion of trade and economic relations between the parties, provide a basis for Community technical and financial assistance, and an appropriate framework to support Slovenia's gradual integration into the Union. The institutional framework of the Europe Agreement provides a mechanism for implementation, management and monitoring of all areas of relations. Sub-committees examine questions at a technical level. The Association Committee, at senior official level, provides for discussion of matters and often finds solutions to problems arising under the Europe Agreement. The Association Council examines the overall status of and perspectives for relations and provides the opportunity to review Slovenia's progress on preparation for accession.

As regards ratification of the Europe Agreement, the Constitutional Court ruled on 5 June 1997 that a prior amendment of the Constitution was necessary before this could take place. The Government of Slovenia has committed itself to obtaining the necessary modification of the Constitution in order to ratify the agreement as soon as possible.

Recognising the need for effective management of the European integration process, the Slovene Government decided on 25 October 1996 to delegate the task of pre-accession policy coordination and monitoring to the Office for European Affairs under the Ministry of Foreign Affairs. Management of the PHARE Programme has also been transferred to the Office.

Pre-Accession Strategy

Implementation of the Interim and Cooperation Agreement and the White Paper

The trade provisions of the Interim Agreement have been implemented according to schedule. The first formal consultations under the Joint/Cooperation Committee were held on 20 and 21 March 1997. Nine sub-committees were established and cooperation at this level has advanced well since then.

Currently, the main issues discussed are: further strengthening the Slovene accession strategy, approximation of legislation; public administration reform; macroeconomic stability and structural reforms; financial services and the liberalisation of capital movements; the wine and spirits agreement; plant health/veterinary equivalency protocol; a European Conformity Assessment Agreement; certification and standardisation issues; a number of specific trade issues; opening of and preparation for participating in community programmes; third-pillar cooperation.

Most of the trade issues which have arisen so far are of minor importance. Given the delayed entry into affect of the Europe Agreement, there is scope for accelerating introduction of policies and mechanisms even ahead of the benchmarks set by the agreements, as for instance in the cases of standards, competition and state aids. Policies, e.g. on aspects of public procurement and movement of capital, have not always been developed in line with the spirit of the Europe Agreement, but in these cases the Government is reviewing its approach in the context of the accession strategy.

The Commission's White Paper of 1995 set out the legislation which the candidate countries would need to transpose and implement in order to apply the *acquis*, and identified elements essential to the implementation of the Single Market (known as Stage I measures) which would need priority attention. Slovenia has attached considerable importance to this work. The Office for European Affairs is supervising the implementation of the White Paper. In addition, the Office for Legislation is responsible for the coordination and monitoring of the working groups in the ministries concerned working on the White Paper implementation. Considering the implementation of the White Paper as a medium-term strategic objective, the Government submitted a three year plan for the approximation of primary legislation in May 1996. It is intended to elaborate this document further, mainly by integrating into it technical standards and secondary legislation, to become a White Paper Implementation Strategy. The strategy is scheduled to be approved before the end of 1997.

Particular progress in legislative alignment has been achieved in the area of banking, intellectual and industrial property, money laundering, consumer protection, personal data, and customs. Areas requiring specific attention are free movement of capital, indirect taxation, insurance, standards, competition and state aids, energy and telecommunication.

Overall, the EC/Slovene Interim Agreement is functioning well. There are no major problems concerning its current implementation. Initial experience of the bilateral consultation mechanism suggests that Slovenia is committed to using it effectively.

Structured Dialogue

Slovenia has participated since June 1996 in the Structured Dialogue. It attaches importance to the dialogue and has made a particular contribution on economic and financial affairs, internal market and energy. The Slovene authorities have expressed satisfaction about the recently introduced long-term planning of meetings and the improved quality of contributions which follows from the longer preparation.

PHARE

Under the PHARE Programme, between 1992 and 1996 Slovenia received 94 million ECU in support of its transformation and pre-accession efforts. The allocation for 1997 was 22 million ECU. There are also cross-border cooperation programmes with Italy (10 million ECU) and Austria (6 million ECU) focusing in particular on economic, environment and infrastructure cooperation.

In the first years PHARE was used mainly for supporting privatisation and enterprise restructuring, reforms in the banking sector and strengthening the Slovene research and development capacity. Later, other targets were added: approximation of legislation, the public administration reform and other fields related to adoption of the *acquis* and fostering of a competitive enterprise sector.

Slovenia has made effective use of PHARE funds. In particular, the Government has targeted a high proportion of technical assistance support at solving specific technical problems related to policy reform, transition, the adoption of the *acquis* and the generation of know-how not accessible in the country. Disbursement rates have been high.

Participation in Community Programmes

Pending ratification of the Europe Agreement, Slovenia is not yet in a position to participate in those Community programmes that need to await establishment of an Association Council.

Trade Relations

Between 1992 and 1996, trade between the EU and Slovenia increased substantially. EU imports from Slovenia jumped from 1,6 to 4,2 billion ECU, while EU exports to Slovenia increased from 1,4 to 5,3 billion. The trade balance developed from a slight surplus in 1992 to a deficit for Slovenia. The deficit increased in 1995 mainly due to the accession to the EU of Austria, Finland and Sweden, and to the need to re-equip the Slovene economy. While Slovene exports represent about 60 % of GDP, approximately 66 % of external trade was with the European Union in 1996. The most important goods traded in both directions were electrical and transport equipment and textiles.

Germany is Slovenia's most important trading partner. In 1996, Germany secured 25,9 % of total Slovene foreign trade, followed by Italy, France, Croatia and Austria. Since independence Slovenia has participated in regional organisations aiming at political stability and economic cooperation. Slovenia is a member of both the Central European Initiative (CEI), and the Central Europe Free Trade Agreement (CEFTA).

General Evaluation

The bilateral relationship has overall been constructive and smooth. But the legislative and constitutional issues which have delayed Slovene ratification of the Europe Agreement have constrained the development of the relationship, despite Slovene willingness in many fields to pursue the enhanced levels of cooperation envisaged in the Europe Agreement even before its entry into force.

B — Criteria for Membership

1. Political Criteria

The European Council in Copenhagen decided on a number of 'political' criteria for accession to be met by the candidate countries in Central and Eastern Europe. These countries must have achieved 'stability of institutions guaranteeing democracy, the rule of law, human rights and respect for and protection of minorities'.

In carrying out the assessment required in this connection, the European Commission has drawn on a number of sources of information: answers given by the Slovenian authorities to the questionnaire sent to them by Commission staff in April 1996, bilateral follow-up meetings, reports from Member States' embassies and the Commission's delegation, assessments by international organisations (including the Council of Europe and the OSCE), reports produced by non-governmental organisations, etc.

The following assessment involves a systematic examination of the main ways in which the public authorities are organised and operate, and the steps they have taken to protect fundamental rights. It does not confine itself to a formal description but seeks to assess the extent to which democracy and the rule of law actually operate.

This assessment relates to the situation in June 1997. It does not examine in detail any changes which have taken place since the fall of the Communist regime or which may come about in the future, though it generally takes account of any stated intention to reform a particular sector. The situation of the Government is mentioned here only in passing: it will be examined in greater depth in Chapter 4.

1.1. Democracy and the Rule of Law

When Slovenia declared independence in June 1991 its Parliament adopted a new Constitution which established parliamentary democracy. The Constitution took effect in December of that year once it had been approved by the country's institutions. Those institutions are working smoothly and normally. The different authorities are mindful of the limits to their powers and of the need cooperate with each other.

Parliament and Legislative Powers: Structure

Parliament is made up of a single chamber, the National Assembly, which has 90 members who are elected for a four-year term under an electoral system which is a blend of proportional representation and simple majority. The Italian and Hungarian minorities each have one seat reserved for them. Slovenia also has a National Council, which represents the interests of socio-economic and professional circles and those of the local authorities. It has 40 members elected for a five-year term. They may give their opinion on draft legislation examined by the National Assembly, call on the latter to have a fresh debate on a draft law before it is promulgated (a majority of the Assembly's members must then vote in favour of the law) and ask for a parliamentary commission of inquiry to be set up.

The President of the Republic has to dissolve the National Assembly if it fails to designate a Prime Minister.

MPs enjoy the usual parliamentary immunities. The Opposition's role and involvement in the working of the country's institutions is recognised, notably through commissions of inquiry which are set up by decision of one-third of the National Assembly's members and have the same powers of investigation as the courts. There are currently six such committees but their effectiveness is questionable in the light of the reports they have produced. The National Assembly also has 39 standing committees but moves are afoot to cut their number to 15.

Slovenia has a multiparty system. Thirty political parties are registered, all of which fielded candidates at the last general elections in 1996. There are no obstacles to the creation of parties, which receive state funding in proportion to the number of votes they obtained at the last elections.

Parliament exercises legislative power and shares the right of initiative with the Government, at least 5 000 electors and the National Council. The legislative process in Slovenia is quite lengthy: once a law has been scrutinised by the relevant standing committee and by the National Council, it must undergo three readings in the National Assembly before the latter can give it final approval.

The Government has autonomous regulatory power which enables it to issue regulations even if the law does not give it prior authorisation. It cannot however issue regulations regarding the rights of individuals or legal persons unless the power to legislate has been delegated to it. The Constitutional Court exercises strict control to ensure that any delegation of powers accorded by Parliament is an express one and that acts issued by the regulatory authority actually correspond to the legislator's intention. The President may pass acts with the force of law in the event of war or a state of emergency or if Parliament cannot assemble (Article 108 of the Constitution), provided such acts are transmitted to Parliament as soon as possible.

The National Assembly may decide to hold a referendum on any matter which seems to merit this, at the request of one-third of its members, or of the National Council or of 40 000 electors. Slovenia held a referendum in November 1996 on the reform of the electoral system for general elections but none of the three changes proposed obtained the required majority.

Functioning of Parliament

The 1992 and 1996 elections were free and fair, each resulting in the formation of coalition governments (see Annex for 1996 results).

Parliament functions satisfactorily: its powers are respected and the Opposition fulfils its proper role. The rules of legislative procedure need to be speeded up, however, and more generally the National Assembly's technical means and staff need to be increased to enable it to fulfil its legislative functions, notably in the context of European integration.

The Executive: Structure

The President of the Republic is elected by direct universal suffrage for a renewable five-year term of office. He has the usual powers accorded to a head of state. If he acts contrary to the Constitution or to the country's laws the National Assembly may call on the Constitutional Court to strip him of his mandate by a two-thirds majority decision of its judges.

The Prime Minister is elected by the Parliament upon a proposal by the President of the Republic. Ministers are also elected by the National Assembly, upon a proposal by the Prime Minister. The Government is answerable to the National Assembly, as is each minister individually.

Local government is run by 58 local government authorities whose leaders are appointed by the Government upon a proposal by the Minister for the Interior. The local government authorities carry out decisions taken by central government and oversee the activity of the local authorities. Their heads are answerable to the Minister of the Interior.

There is only one category of local authority in Slovenia, the municipality, the number of which was increased in 1994 from 62 to 147 (20 new ones are planned). The municipalities administer the bulk of local public services and are run by a mayor, who is elected by direct universal suffrage, and by a municipal council also elected for a four-year term of office. Government subsidies continue to form a substantial part of the municipalities' budget resources and several draft laws are in the pipeline to afford them a greater measure of financial autonomy.

Public administration in Slovenia is governed by two laws: one affecting government and parliamentary officials and another governing the employees of government agencies which lays down rules akin to those contained in the Labour Code. Although the Constitution provides for it, there is no law at present guaranteeing openness in measures taken by the administration.

The army, the secret services and the police are under civilian control. In 1996 a start was made on reorganising the police at local level to enhance its effectiveness. The army is under the control of Parliament and the executive. The Prime Minister is directly responsible for the activities of the secret services.

Functioning of the Executive

Central government works normally and smoothly.

As Slovenia became independent only recently, the development of local government is still under way. The government reform programme provides for the transfer of new powers to the municipalities. A law on the reform of local authorities is being examined by Parliament.

To make the administration more effective the Government is planning a comprehensive programme to modernise the legal, administrative, financial and organisational aspects of public administration and to boost the training of officials. The fight against corruption is another prime objective.

The parliamentary committee responsible for controlling the activities of the police has run up against a number of obstacles in carrying out its tasks, notably owing to the sometimes fraught relations with the Ministry for the Interior. Nonetheless, control of the police's activities and the scope for calling it to account are satisfactory.

The Judiciary: Structure

The judiciary is independent of the other branches of government. Judges are appointed for life by the National Assembly upon a proposal by the 'Judicial Council', the body responsible for administering the Bench. It is made up of 11 members, five of whom are elected by Parliament upon a proposal from the President of the Republic while the six others are selected from among sitting judges. The judges may only be relieved of their functions by the National Assembly upon a proposal by the Judicial Council, if they have committed a crime in carrying out their functions, or if they have been sentenced to a term of imprisonment lasting more than six months. They enjoy immunity and may not be detained unless Parliament has given prior authorisation. In common with the prosecutors, the judges enjoy freedom of expression and freedom of association.

The department of public prosecutions is independent of the legislature and the executive. The Prosecutor General is appointed for six years by Parliament upon a proposal from the Government. The National Assembly may also dismiss the Prosecutor General by a simple majority vote.

Article 25 of the Constitution enshrines the right to contest the actions taken by the administration. However, in practice, the only appellate body is the specialised chamber of the Supreme Court which is currently very congested owing to the number of cases brought before it, notably since the development of local autonomy. Moreover, the procedure before the Court is entirely written and cases are not judged during public audience. As a result, the Government has decided to create a genuine administrative jurisdiction comprising four courts whose decisions, taken following a public audience, can be contested before the Supreme Court. This Bill is still being examined by Parliament.

In September 1994 Slovenia created the office of ombudsman elected by the National Assembly. The ombudsman's task is to examine complaints sent to him. So far he has mainly been called on to intervene by persons in prison or in detention centres.

The Constitutional Court is composed of nine judges appointed by Parliament for a non-renewable nine-year term of office upon a proposal from the President of the Republic. The Court ensures that laws, decrees and regulatory acts issued by local authorities are consistent with the Constitution, international treaties and the general principles of international law. It also rules on requests from appellants who feel that their fundamental rights enshrined in the Constitution have been violated. Pursuant to Article 162 of the Constitution any person who can demonstrate that he or she has a case to bring may bring it before the court. The President of the Republic, the Government or one-third of the members of the National Assembly may ask the court to rule on whether an international treaty to be ratified is consistent with the Constitution.

Functioning of the Judiciary

The main problems facing the Slovenian judiciary are inefficiency and the amount of time it takes to hand down judgments: it can take five years before a civil case is brought before the courts. Slovenia lacks judges notably as a result of the relatively low level of pay and the statutory requirement that they must be at least 30 years of age. This situation should be improved as a result of the programme to equip courts with computers and the planned procedural reforms.

The Constitutional Court plays an important role in the functioning of the institutions and democracy in Slovenia. Its case law has helped bolster the establishment of the rule of law by giving certain guidelines to other courts in applying the many new laws. Since it was created the Court has examined some 1 500 cases, 80 % of which have been brought by private individuals. Around 5 % have been upheld.

1.2. Human Rights and the Protection of Minorities

Slovenia has put in place a number of regulations to guarantee the respect of human rights and the rights of minorities. These rights can also be underpinned by certain international conventions, foremost of which is the European Convention for the Protection of Human Rights and its main additional protocols. Taken as a whole, this constitutes — pursuant to Article F of the Treaty on European Union — part of the *acquis* any state wishing to join the European Union must first have ratified these texts.

Slovenia, which has been a member of the Council of Europe since May 1993, ratified the European Convention for the Protection of Human Rights and the additional protocols in June 1994. Individuals may take their case to the European Court if they consider that their rights under this Convention have been violated.

Among the other international conventions protecting human rights and minorities, Slovenia has ratified the European Convention on the Prevention of Torture, but has yet to ratify the Framework Convention on Minorities or sign the European Social Charter. It has ratified the key UN conventions in the field of human rights.

Pursuant to Article 8 of the Constitution, Slovenian laws should be consistent with international treaties which have a direct effect on domestic law.

Civil and Political Rights

Access to justice is largely guaranteed in Slovenia. A legal aid system applies to the criminal courts. The legal security of citizens is hampered only by the length of time taken to deliver judgments.

The death penalty has been abolished and Slovenia ratified Protocol No 6 of the European Human Rights Convention in June 1994.

The right not to be arbitrarily arrested is guaranteed: under Article 20 of the Constitution any arrest needs a prior decision of a court. Any person arrested must be notified of the reason within 24 hours. The maximum period of detention is three months. Article 30 of the Constitution affords any person arrested unjustly the right to compensation.

All citizens aged 18 and over have the right to vote.

Freedom of association and assembly are guaranteed. The dynamism of the voluntary sector, which was allowed to operate even before 1991, is reflected in the existence of around 2 000 NGOs in Slovenia.

Freedom of expression is guaranteed. The press has been privatised and journalists no longer encounter obstacles in exercising their profession. In the audio-visual field, the public channels (three radio and two television) have private-sector competitors (three national television channels and myriad national and local radio stations). Most households can receive foreign radio and TV stations. During election campaigns all the political parties are entitled to equal air time on radio and television to put across their programme.

The right of ownership is recognised by the Constitution. However, foreigners are still subject to certain limitations, notably as regards ownership of land, which is only permitted through inheritance and only where there is reciprocity for Slovenian citizens in the country of origin of the foreign national in question (Article 68 of the Constitution).

In its opinion of 5 June 1997, the Constitutional Court confirmed that ratification of the Europe Agreement required prior amendment of Article 68 of the Constitution and the legal arrangements currently in force. The Government undertook to carry out these amendments as soon as possible.

The process of returning property to persons dispossessed by the Communist regime is painfully slow, with only 50 % of disputes having been settled and 10 % of real estate restored to the rightful owner. The Constitutional Court cancelled the moratorium decided in December 1995 on the return of properties in excess of 200 hectares. In order to avoid fresh difficulties occurring in the implementation of this legislation and to reduce any uncertainty in the situation as regards property rights, Parliament must adopt the necessary rules, and the procedures under way will have to be speeded up. This operation will be facilitated by the implementation and computerisation of the land registry which is to be carried out in 1998.

The dispute with Italy on the return of certain property confiscated at the end of the Second World War will be settled by the provisions of Annex XIII to the Europe Agreement, which also covers the issue of acquisition of real estate in Slovenia by EU citizens.

Respect for privacy is safeguarded by the need for a judge's warrant to be issued prior to a house search or telephone tapping. Article 36.4 of the Constitution allows the authorities to derogate from this rule in cases of absolute necessity. This procedure has not thus far given rise to abuse on the part of the police.

Slovenia has ratified the Geneva Convention on Refugees and is working on an amendment to its domestic legislation to bring it into line with EU rules. There are currently around 8 700 refugees from the former Yugoslavia taking advantage of temporary protection measures.

No cases of inhuman and degrading treatment have been reported.

The Slovenian authorities have not yet settled nationality issues arising from the break-up of the former Yugoslavia. Persons residing permanently on Slovenian territory and wishing to obtain Slovenian nationality had until 25 December 1991 to do so. More than 98 % of applicants obtained it. Since then, 16 000 new applications have been lodged; 6 000 were accepted and 900 rejected. An issue still to be resolved concerns a group of around 5 000 stateless people who for various reasons have neither asked for Slovenian nationality nor claimed refugee status. The Government will be taking appropriate steps to resolve this problem.

Economic, Social and Cultural Rights

The right to social security is recognised by the Constitution (Article 50 and Article 52 for those with no income).

Freedom to belong to a trade union is guaranteed by Article 76. Four federations embrace the vast majority of Slovenians belonging to a trade union. Membership stands at around 50 %. The right to strike is recognised in Article 77. The law can, however, curtail this right if this is in the public interest, taking into account the activity of the sector concerned.

The Constitution also guarantees freedom of education and religion. A dispute has arisen between the Government and the Roman Catholic church on the issue of the return of property confiscated by the Communist regime. The above-mentioned decision of the Constitutional Court should resolve the matter.

Minority Rights and the Protection of Minorities

Minorities in Slovenia account for around 8 % of the population (2,8 % Croats, 2,4 % Serbs, 1,4 % Bosnians, 0,43 % Hungarians and 0,16 % Italians). Only the Hungarians and Italians are recognised as minorities because the other groups are not settled permanently in Slovenia.

The Constitution recognises the rights of minorities. Each group is represented by a deputy in the National Assembly who has the power to block the adoption of laws which concern the exercise of the specific rights of those communities or their status. The minorities have the right to form their own autonomous institutions at local level for putting into practice the rights which have been accorded to them in the educational, cultural and information fields. The Italian and Hungarian communities also have the right to promote their ties with Italy and Hungary. Article 62 of the Constitution recognises the right of individuals to use their own language in dealings with the administration.

Article 65 of the Constitution also recognises the special nature of the Roma (gypsy) community, which numbers around 7 000 - 10 000 people. A special law on the protection of gypsies is currently under scrutiny by the National Assembly and in 1995 the Slovenian Government implemented a programme to strengthen the application of their social and political rights. They are represented in the municipal councils of the towns in which they live.

1.3. General Evaluation

The Slovenian institutions work smoothly, the various authorities being mindful of the limits of their powers and of the need for cooperation. The 1992 and 1996 elections were free and fair. The opposition fulfills a normal role in the operation of the institutions.

There are no major problems regarding observance of fundamental rights in the country. The rights of minorities are guaranteed and protected. Certain improvements still need to be made in terms of the working of the judicial system and the restoration to the original owners of property expropriated by the Communist regime. Efforts to combat corruption need to be more effective.

Slovenia is a democracy with stable institutions which guarantee the rule of law, human rights and respect for, and the protection of, minorities.

2. Economic Criteria

In examining the economic situation and prospects of Slovenia, the Commission's approach is guided in particular by the conclusions of the European Council in Copenhagen in June 1993, which stated that membership of the Union requires 'the existence of a functioning market economy, as well as the capacity to cope with competitive pressure and market forces within the Union'.

This chapter of the Opinion therefore gives a concise survey of the economic situation and background, followed by a review of Slovenia's progress in key areas of economic transformation (liberalisation of the price and trade system, stabilisation of the economy, structural change, reform of the financial sector) as well as its economic and social development. It concludes with a general evaluation of Slovenia in relation to the criteria mentioned by the European Council and a review of prospects and priorities for further reform.

2.1. Economic Situation

Background

Slovenia, with a population of 2 million, has a gross domestic product (GDP) of 20 billion ECU

(expressed in purchasing power parity); its population is about 0,5 % of that of the Union, while its economy is only about 0,3 %. GDP per head is about 59 % of the Union average. The average net monthly wage is around 475 ECU.

Slovenia was a founding member of the WTO in 1995, and joined CEFTA in 1996.

Progress in Economic Transformation

Slovenia already started to develop as an industrialised economy while it was part of the Habsburg empire, until 1918. It then became part of Yugoslavia, which turned communist in 1945. The country adopted a socialist system with self-management and social ownership complimentary to central planning and state ownership. During the 1980s the imbalances produced by the system became apparent: income began to fall and inflation to rise. There was a build-up of debt which Slovenia could not easily manage due to lack of access to new loans from abroad, and significant transfers to other republics. Some attempts at reform were made before independence in 1991, but progress was limited.

Slovenia had always been the wealthiest and most open of the former Yugoslav republics, benefiting from an advantageous geographical location and a prosperous past. By 1990, while it only accounted for 9 % of the Yugoslav population, it produced about 16 % of output and accounted for 27 % of foreign trade. In 1991 Slovenia achieved independence and began to transform the economy. As Slovenia had never been subject to the typical command planning, the degree of centralisation was lower than elsewhere in central Europe. It was also less dependent on the Soviet Union. However, as in other transition economies there were a number of distortions: there were restrictions on property rights and the use of capital; there was excessive emphasis on heavy industry; large companies played a dominant role; and a substantial share of trade was directed towards communist countries.

At the beginning of transition, emphasis was put on stabilisation, rather than reform. Although trade and some prices were liberalised early on, fiscal reform, privatisation and restructuring came later and still have some way to go.

Small-scale private activity was permitted under Yugoslav law, and state ownership was relatively limited. The main form of ownership was 'social' ownership where management was relatively independent, rather than being controlled from the centre, and worker involvement in the running of enterprises was strong. Nevertheless, certain distortions associated with command planning were evident: a lack of financial discipline leading to lower quality and less efficient production and over-employment. Indeed, jobs were guaranteed and labour shedding was banned.

Privatisation and the birth of new enterprises have led to an increase in the role of the private sector. Privatisation has focused on socially-owned enterprises, while the privatisation of state-owned enterprises still has to be dealt with.

Foreign Direct Investment

Foreign direct investment in Slovenia has remained low compared to the size of the economy: annual inflows have never surpassed 1 % of GDP (source: EBRD). The main reasons for this are the small size of the market, the preferential treatment of domestic investors during the privatisation process, and an incomplete legal framework. In recent years, few completely new inward investments were made, and foreign direct investment flows went mainly to enterprises which already had existing foreign partnerships.

Economic Structure

The role of *agriculture*, in terms of contributions to output, is very much like in the EU; it accounts for about 5 % of value added. However, it accounts for a larger share of employment: around 7 %. Apart from competitive estates in the north-east of the country, efficiency is low and structures are fragmented. Most agricultural land had remained in private hands during communism, so transition problems were not so pronounced. Slovenia is a net importer of food and agricultural products. Subsidies are important, mainly for mountainous regions.

The structure of the economy changed as a result of the break up of the former Yugoslavia and CMEA, and the stabilisation programme: *industry's* share in employment and output dropped to 35 % and 33 % respectively by 1993. Industrial production growth has not been consistently strong since then; in 1996 it virtually stagnated. Industry accounted for 32 % of GDP in 1995 — with manufacturing accounting for 28 %. The main production area is manufacture of metal products. However, the industrial structure is relatively flat — there is less specialisation than might be expected of a small, open economy. The most dynamic areas in 1995 where the manufacture of transport and electrical equipment, while in 1996 the most dynamic were textiles and food processing.

The relative importance of *services* as a whole has increased, partly because industry contracted but also because tourism has expanded. This has been a major growth area.

There is evidence on the existence of a significant *shadow economy* in Slovenia. The most visual indication of this is the extent of undeclared employment: while recorded unemployment is over 14 %, according to the labour market survey (using ILO methodology) actual unemployment is only around 7 %. The notable growth of undeclared employment in temporary or contract work or as family workers is mainly due to high non-wage labour costs.

Main indicators of economic structure

(All data for 1996 unless otherwise indicated)

Population	in million	2.0
GDP per head	in PPS-ECU (1995)	10 100
as % of EU-15 average	in per cent (1995)	59
Share of agriculture in:		
— gross value added	in per cent (1995)	5
— employment	in per cent (1995)	7.1
Gross foreign debt/GDP	in per cent	22
Exports of goods and services/GDP	in per cent (1995)	55
Stock of foreign direct investment[1]	in billion ECU	0.6
	in ECU per head	290

Source: Commission services, national sources, EBRD.
[1] FDI stock converted at end-1996 exchange rate of 1 ECU = $1,25299.

Liberalisation

Price Regime

The vast majority of prices have been liberalised, but prices of certain key commodities, such as energy, telecommunications and transport, are still administered. They form a significant part in household consumption, accounting for some 26 % of the goods and services in the price index basket. Because at their current levels administered prices do not necessarily cover the production costs, their adjustment over the coming years will contribute to inflation.

Direct budget subsidies are quite limited, and exist only on certain foodstuffs and public services: in total they amount to about 3 % of the budget. In addition, some of the larger enterprises receive support from the Development Fund, which was originally set up to provide emergency funding to stabilize enterprises that were salvageable or initiate winding-up procedures for those that had no realistic prospects of survival.

Trade Regime

Trade was liberalised at the outset. Most quantitative restrictions have been removed. Some non-tariff barriers remain but the Government is committed to removing them in sectors such as telecommunications and electrical equipment. The weighted average tariff rate applied to most-favoured nations stood at 10,7 % in 1996. Most of the international trade is still invoiced in either DM or $, rather than in the domestic currency.

Foreign Exchange Regime

The currency, the tolar, was introduced in 1991. The government accepted the obligations of the IMF Article VIII in 1995, although the currency had been *de facto* convertible for current account purposes from early 1992. At first the currency was allowed to float freely, during which time it depreciated heavily. As the currency began to stabilize and inflation dropped sharply, the Bank of Slovenia adopted a managed float. The aim was to keep the real exchange rate stable and bring down inflation in order to protect competitiveness and help boost output. The system was also chosen because Slovenia has a small monetary base so it is very susceptible to swings in capital inflows. From mid-1992, these increased as a result of current account surpluses. These inflows were sterilised, at a considerable cost, to contain money supply growth and hence inflationary pressure. The policy seems to have been relatively successful. However, due to the costs of sterilisation, the Bank of Slovenia had to gradually restrict capital inflows to be able to maintain the chosen policy objectives.

Liberalisation of capital flows has made slow progress: capital outflows are generally subject to authorisation while the capital inflow regime has recently become more restrictive. A particular grey area is that of operations in securities.

Stabilisation of the Economy

Domestic

As in other transition economies, there was a fall in output due to the collapse of CMEA (Yugoslavia was not a full member, but CMEA still accounted for a substantial amount of trade), the break-up of Yugoslavia, and the transformation process. In addition, price liberalisation and the release of forced savings accumulated under the old system initially led to rapid inflation, and unemployment soared as industry shed workers. However, the impact of the decline was less dramatic than elsewhere because Slovenia had long-established access to western markets, so trade re-orientation was less dramatic, and the starting level of output was somewhat higher.

The recovery began in 1993 and was stimulated largely by favourable economic developments in the European export markets. However, rapid GDP growth concealed some domestic weaknesses, such as high wage growth and delays in structural reforms. Consequently, when economic growth in Europe slowed down in 1995, this was immediately reflected in lower economic growth and higher unemployment in Slovenia. This process was further reinforced by a simultaneous appreciation of the tolar. Since the middle of 1996, the situation has begun to improve again. Higher growth in domestic demand, improved competitiveness, and the first signs of economic recovery in the EU, resulted in an improving growth performance in the second half of the year. Nevertheless, GDP growth in 1996 (3,1 %) remained slightly lower than in 1995. The above mentioned positive growth factors should remain present in the near future, and an acceleration of growth to 4-5 % can be expected.

On the fiscal side, Slovenia benefited from the break-up of Yugoslavia because it had been a net contributor to the federal budget. While tax revenues were maintained, the transfers to the other republics decreased, so the budget has, until now, remained approximately in equilibrium. However, deficits in the pension system, higher social security expenditure, reduced customs revenues as a consequence of European integration, and a rising public wage bill, could result in a deterioration of the fiscal balance in the near future if reforms are not implemented. Given the tight monetary policy framework, a significant government deficit would crowd out private investment.

External

In June 1995, the question of the unresolved allocation of ex-Yugoslavia's foreign debt, was settled as Slovenia took on a share of ex-Yugoslav liabilities. Even with this additional debt, the overall debt level remains modest: gross debt at then end of 1996 was 3,2 billion ECU, which is fully covered by gross reserves of 3,3 billion ECU.

The economic fortunes of Slovenia are very tied in with its external performance, which in turn is dependent on its ability to remain competitive. Exports of goods and services account for some 55 % of GDP, and although there is a trade deficit, the receipts from tourism kept the current account in surplus, with the exception of

Main economic trends

		1994	1995	1996
Real GDP growth rate	in per cent	5.3	3.9	3.1
Inflation rate				
— annual average	in per cent	19.8	12.6	9.7
— December on December	in per cent	19.5	8.9	9.1
Unemployment rate, end-year	in per cent ILO definition	9	7.4	7.3
General government budget balance	in per cent of GDP	−0.2	0.0	0.1
Current account balance	in per cent of GDP	3.7	−0.2	0.3
Debt/export ratio	in per cent	26.5	29.0	38.2
Foreign direct investment inflow	in per cent of GDP	0.9	0.9	0.8

Source: Commission services, national sources, EBRD.

1995 when a small deficit was recorded. As a result, the country's foreign exchange reserves have increased steadily, having been non-existent at the beginning of transition.

Structural Change

Foreign Trade

Trade with the EU has always been relatively significant, but has increased since independence: almost 65 % of all trade went to the EU in 1996. The most important trading partners are Germany, Italy and France. After a sharp fall in the first years of transition, the share of trade with the other countries of former Yugoslavia is now increasing again, as a result of the stabilisation in the region. The importance of CEFTA countries in Slovenia's trade has also been increasing after Slovenia became a member, while the shares of Russia and the rest of former Soviet Union have been falling. Trade re-orientation has therefore largely taken place.

The commodity composition of exports and imports has not changed significantly as a result of transition. Consumer goods are the most significant export category, while investment and intermediate goods dominate imports. Merchandise trade is highly concentrated: 83 % of exports and 67 % of imports are manufactured goods or machinery. Within this, machinery and transport equipment alone account for one third of total exports.

Slovenia has the competitive advantages of low wages compared to the EU, and highly skilled workers. To remain competitive, given the rising wages, quality and productivity improvements are increasingly important. More foreign direct investment will be needed to provide the necessary capital and know-how.

Labour Market

In Slovenia, labour costs are relatively high for a transition economy and the labour market is quite inflexible. The main reasons are that a) the payroll is the main source of tax revenue, so labour, as opposed to profits and consumption, bears a disproportionate share of the tax burden; b) there is a rigid system of collective and social agreements; c) the levels of redundancy pay-

ments are very high; d) strong links between workers and management exist — both under the old regime and since the management/employee buy-outs during privatisation — which have hampered labour market adjustment by allowing rapid wage growth and the persistence of over-staffing in certain areas.

Under the previous regime lay-offs were actually banned. In 1988/1989 legislation was passed to make lay-offs possible. However, the cost of the obligatory compensation that had to be paid to redundant workers was prohibitive. The Government has sought to reduce these, but there is some way to go yet. Social security contributions have also been reduced but total labour costs remain 50-60 % higher than the average gross wage.

Statistics show that employment in socially-owned enterprises fell dramatically in the early 1990s. However, this includes a large number of workers transferred to private subsidiaries, suggesting that working practices may not have changed that significantly. Despite the decline of industry and the increased importance of smaller firms, employment is still dominated by large-scale heavy industry.

The wage distribution in Slovenia is quite flat. This is partly due to an egalitarian tradition reinforced by a long history of worker management. This has led to relatively high wages — which are indexed anyway — at the expense of profits, and to high employment. Real wages actually increased in 1992 and 1993, despite the decline in GDP; this put extreme pressure on competitiveness, and forced some wage capping. The first Social Agreement between employers, the government and the unions, intended to contain wage growth, was signed in 1994. As the pressure on wages remained strong subsequently, follow-up agreements were signed in 1995 and 1996. The Social Agreements have had only limited restraining effects: real wage growth in 1996 was still at 5 %, well above the intended 1,5 % under the Agreement.

The minimum wage is fairly generous, and under current rules it will remain so as it is indexed to inflation every quarter: in June 1996 it stood at 53 500 tolar (42 % of the average commercial sector wage).

Public Finances

As Slovenia was paying significant transfers to the other republics in Yugoslavia, the budgetary position improved with independence in 1991. Nevertheless a substantial amount of reform was necessary to support the new role of Government — in a market economy and following independence. Most of this has already taken place.

On the revenue side, in 1993, personal income and corporate profits taxes were introduced. However, Value Added Tax has not yet been introduced — and is now expected to be in place only in 1999. Recently, the tax pressure on labour has been lowered by a reduction of social security contributions by employers. However, this reduction has not yet been fully compensated by other measures, so that the budget is expected to record a significant deficit in 1997.

On the expenditure side, the share of transfers to enterprises and households has fallen. Meanwhile the social security system has been reformed to provide a social safety net. However, the pension and unemployment funds are running ever higher deficits, which are being covered by the state budget. They will therefore need further reform to make them financially sustainable.

In addition to central and local government spending, there are a number of extra-budgetary funds. The most important of these are the health and pension funds, but there is a growing number of smaller funds. At present they do not operate under a unified legal framework, which reduces fiscal transparency and could put the overall budget position at risk.

Enterprise Sector: Privatisation and Enterprise Restructuring

The existence of private enterprises has been possible since 1988. Entry into the market was not exclusively dictated by the State and market prices prevailed in many areas. However, a significant amount of privatisation and measures to boost the development of small and medium-sized firms were needed. The private sector currently accounts for only 50-55 % of output and employment.

Under the previous regime, the system of socially-owned enterprises and worker management meant that the distinction between owners, managers and workers was not clear: in most enterprises managers were appointed by the employees. In larger enterprises, the authorities nominated them. The problems of self-interest led to wage escalation, over-employment and under-investment. Loss-making enterprises survived not so much because of government subsidies but because they accumulated arrears to other enterprises, and they had easy access to bank loans — which in turn undermined the health of the banking sector.

Since mid-1993 the authorities have given priority to the financial restructuring of socially-owned enterprises. This was mainly done through the Development Fund. The task of the development fund is to restructure, sell or close industrial enterprises that could not be privatised. More recently, the fund is supporting some of the larger enterprises that are still loss-making. The main problem faced by the fund is the limited financial resources available for its operations. Another primary objective of the Government has been to encourage private sector development through legal reforms and the introduction of a regulatory framework adapted to the market economy.

Privatisation of the socially-owned enterprises progressed rather slowly until late in 1994, but is expected to be completed by the end of 1997. All citizens of Slovenia were given free non-transferable certificates in 1994 (equivalent to 40 % of the total social capital of all the enterprises), which they can use to buy shares in companies or in investment trusts. The Government, eager to speed up privatisation, granted the Privatisation Agency control over the privatisation of every company which has not yet started work on privatisation plans. One remaining problem will be the 'privatisation gap', which is caused by the fact that the value of the issued vouchers exceeds the value of the assets to be privatised by about one third. There is currently no decision on which of the remaining state assets will be privatised against vouchers to bridge the gap.

State-owned enterprises (utilities and other monopolies) continue to represent an important part of the enterprise sector. In 1995, they still represented more than 30 % of the assets of all larger enterprises (having more than ten employees and surpassing certain thresholds on assets and revenues). Their statutory regulations remain unclear, and there is a lack of effective monitoring and control structures.

The current enterprise structure has not developed much since independence: the system is still dominated by some large firms. In 1995, small enterprises (0-50 employees) accounted for 8 % of manufacturing output while the larger enterprises (251+ employees) accounted for 69 %. Large firms also understandably dominate in exports: they accounted for 76 % of manufacturing exports in 1995.

Foreign investment has been slow to develop in Slovenia, compared to the size of the economy. This is largely due to two factors. Firstly, privatisation progressed slowly. Secondly, management and employee buy-outs were common, which made it harder for outsiders to gain access to shares — in fact, by end-1995, in 78 % of the companies that had completed privatisation, its employees held 60 % or more of the shares. These are the smaller companies. Employees could not afford to buy up the larger firms, so there is more foreign participation in these. Where there is foreign investment, profitability has generally improved.

Further restructuring of firms is needed to reduce the drain on public resources, including on the Development Fund, and to prevent crowding-out of profitable firms. Changes have been slow in coming because of the links between banks and the possibility of running up inter-enterprise arrears. In addition, the amount of new investment has been limited by high interest rates, which makes that the returns on capital are low.

Financial Sector

The Bank of Slovenia is responsible for monetary and exchange rate policy. It was created in 1991 as an independent authority to maintain national currency stability. It targets the money supply, and controls it through the use of indirect instruments, such as open market operations, required reserves and refinancing credits. It has been relatively successful in achieving price stability. However, its task is made difficult by the extent of indexation in the economy, most importantly of interest rates and wages.

The banking sector was quite decentralised under the previous regime and there was a substantial bad loans problem. Initially, in the early 1990s, loan portfolios deteriorated due to poor enterprise performance leading to a loss of bank assets. Although the bank rehabilitation programme is now coming to an end, competition is still lacking and banks still have high operational cost levels. Most banks in Slovenia are small and maintain high reserves in conformity with the Central Bank's requirements. The two largest banks are state-owned. In addition, there is an interest rate arrangement between the banks which sets the maximum rates on deposits. This cartel has been approved by the Bank of Slovenia and the anti-monopoly office. It is not compatible with a market-oriented financial system. Abolishing the interest rate cartel, combined with the privatisation of the remaining state banks and a higher foreign involvement in the sector, would force the banks to restructure and increase their competitiveness.

All banks meet the international capital adequacy requirement and the performance of the banking sector has been improving in the recent period. Overall, the profitability of the sector has improved as a result of increased bank earnings and control of costs. Nevertheless, because of the too small scale of the banks, costs remain high by international comparison.

The development of the financial sector, e.g., the money and capital markets, also suffers from the anachronistic payments system inherited from the former Yugoslavia. Although the appropriate legislation has been adopted, the markets are dominated by the main banks and only a limited number of financial instruments are available, so the sector has not deepened. The stock exchange is technologically advanced, but it is small and does not contribute much to the financial markets. The slow start to privatisation has had a part to play in this. The recent introduction of restrictions on portfolio capital inflows has significantly reduced the trading volumes on the stock exchange.

The interbank market is the only organised part of the money market. Commercial banks, enterprises, some state-owned funds, insurance companies and the Government all participate.

Economic and Social Development

Social Indicators

Slovenia is a small country with a population of 2 million. The population has remained very stable over the past decade.

The workforce is skilled and fairly well educated — in particular the younger generations. The share of employed who have received secondary education is relatively high at 60 % (1995). In addition, there is a significant amount of training, both on-the-job and otherwise: the authorities estimate that some 30 % of those employed receive training.

Life expectancy, which was reduced as a result of transition, is currently only slightly below the EU average and rising again: women's life expectancy was 77,4 years and men's was 69,6 in 1994.

Regional and Sectoral Differences

In recent years the level of urbanisation has increased with industrialisation, however, it remains relatively low: in 1995, 50 % of the population lived in cities.

2.2. The Economy in the Perspective of Membership

Introduction

The European Council in Copenhagen in 1993 defined the conditions that the associated countries in Central and Eastern Europe need to satisfy for accession. The economic criteria are:

☐ the existence of a functioning market economy;

☐ the capacity to cope with competitive pressure and market forces within the Union.

These criteria are linked. Firstly, a functioning market economy will be better able to cope with competitive pressure. Secondly, in the context of membership of the Union, the functioning market is the internal market. Without integration into the internal market, EU membership would lose its economic meaning, both for Slovenia and for its partners.

The adoption of the *acquis*, and in particular the internal market *acquis*, is therefore essential for a candidate country, which must commit itself *permanently* to the economic obligations of membership. This irreversible commitment is needed to provide the certainty that every part of the enlarged EU market will continue to operate by common rules.

The capacity to take on the *acquis* has several dimensions. On the one hand, Slovenia needs to be capable of taking on the economic obligations of membership, in such a way that the Single Market functions smoothly and fairly. On the other hand, Slovenia's capacity to benefit fully from the competitive pressures of the internal market requires that the underlying economic environment be favourable, and that the Slovenian economy have flexibility and a sufficient level of human and physical capital, especially infrastructure. In their absence, competitive pressures are likely to be considered too intense by some sections of society, and there will be a call for protective measures, which, if implemented, would undermine the Single Market.

The capacity and determination of a candidate country to adopt and implement the *acquis* will be crucial, since the costs and benefits of doing so may be unevenly spread across time, industries and social groups. The existence of a broad based consensus about the nature of the changes to economic policy which membership of the Union requires, and a sustained record of implementation of economic reforms in the face of interest group pressure reduce the risk that a country will be unable to maintain its commitment to the economic obligations of membership.

At the level of the public authorities, membership of the Union requires the administrative and legal capacity to transpose and implement the wide range of technical legislation needed to remove obstacles to freedom of movement within the Union and so ensure the working of the Single Market. These aspects are examined in later chapters. At the level of individual firms, the impact on their competitiveness of adopting the *acquis* depends on their capacity to adapt to the new economic environment.

Existence of a functioning Market Economy

The existence of a market economy requires that equilibrium between supply and demand is established by the free interplay of market forces. A market economy is functioning when the legal system, including the regulation of property rights, is in place and can be enforced. The performance of a market economy is facilitated and improved by macroeconomic stability and a degree of consensus about the essentials of economic policy. A well-developed financial sector and an absence of significant barriers to market entry and exit help to improve the efficiency with which an economy works.

Slovenia began the transition process from a favourable starting point: it was a relatively wealthy country with some good infrastructure, a history of decentralised decision-making and established links with the West. It had industrialised before becoming communist and it never adopted command planning; private ownership began to develop before independence.

The framework for a market economy is largely in place. Macroeconomic stabilisation has been largely achieved: inflation is in single digits, the budget and the current account are approximately in equilibrium, the currency is stable, and economic growth resumed in 1993. Trade, most prices and the foreign exchange regime have been liberalised, private ownership has been extended, legislation appropriate to a market economy is being passed and property rights are enforced. Good progress in the implementation of the Europe Agreement should help to consolidate the functioning of the market economy.

However, the extent of competition and the degree to which the market mechanisms work still need some improvement: for example, licensing procedures are still very formal, bankruptcy procedures are slow, and a cartel operates in the banking sector. The high degree of indexation in the economy also introduces a significant amount of inertia into the system.

Reform of public finances is also still necessary. In particular, VAT has to be introduced and the tax burden on labour reduced. Social transfers and public wages represent an increasing burden on government expenditure which should be reduced. The most important and the most difficult issue is pensions. Public expenditure on pensions is taking an increasing share of GDP and an increasing amount comes from the central budget. Measures to assure the short-term sustainability of the system will have to be accompanied by more structural reforms.

A strong and stable financial sector is an essential element of a functioning market economy. Although the banking system has a long tradition of decentralisation, and regulation appears effective, the system is still underdeveloped and needs to mature. Interest rate spreads, i.e. the difference between rates on loans and on deposits, are high because many of the banks are too small, and because operating costs are high. In general, the sector lacks competitive pressures to enforce higher competitiveness. As a result, the banking sector is not able to perform its role as a financial intermediary: savings are not being efficiently channelled to productive investment. Nevertheless, the financial sector is certainly sufficiently developed not to hinder the normal functioning of the economy.

Capacity to cope with Competitive Pressure and Market Forces

It is difficult, some years ahead of prospective membership, and before Slovenia has adopted and implemented the larger part of Community law, to form a definitive judgement of the country's ability to fulfil this criterion. Nevertheless, it is possible to identify a number of features of Slovenia's development which provide some indication of its probable capacity to cope with competitive pressure and market forces within the Union.

This requires a stable macroeconomic framework within which individual economic agents can make decisions in a climate of a reasonable degree of predictability. There must be a sufficient amount of human and physical capital including infrastructure to provide the background so that individual firms have the ability to adapt to face increased competitive pressures in the Single Market. Firms need to invest to improve their efficiency, so that they can both compete at home and take advantage of economies of scale which flow from access to the Single Market. This capacity to adapt will be greater, the more firms have access to investment finance, the better the quality of their workforce, and the more successful they are at innovation.

Moreover, an economy will be better able to take on the obligations of membership the higher the degree of economic integration it achieves with the Union ahead of accession. The more integrated a country already is with the Union, the less the further restructuring implied by membership. The level of economic integration is related to both the range and volume of goods traded with Member States. Direct benefits from access to the Single Market may also be greater in sectors where there is a sizeable proportion of small firms, since these are relatively more affected by impediments to trade.

Slovenia is potentially quite capable of coping with the competitive pressure and market forces within the Union. The *stabilisation* of the *macroeconomic environment* is well advanced, *infrastructure* is well developed, and significant progress has been made in reorienting the *education* and *training* system in order to support competitiveness. Although it has traditionally had relatively high labour costs, the economy was able to export successfully because production was of relatively good quality, and unit labour costs were still low relative to the EU. However, the level of competitiveness has been reduced by rapid wage growth and the real appreciation of the currency. Competition from other transition economies, where labour costs are even lower, has been increasing. Although productivity gains have taken place, the slow pace of improvement in competitiveness is hampering the expansion of economic activity.

The high degree of *integration with the Union* — about two thirds of total export and import flows are with the EU — suggests that competitiveness remains quite high. In addition, a more detailed breakdown of exports of goods shows that although transport and electrical equipment account for 25 % of exports, Slovenia successfully exports a relatively wide range of products, which indicates the general ability of the Slovenian economy to compete in the Single Market. Moreover, the current widespread involvement in trade with the EU reduces the vulnerability of the economy to the full integration in the Single Market and the adoption of the *acquis* even if some sector would prove to be unable to withstand the competition within the Single Market after accession, the diversification of exports would leave the economy relatively unharmed.

Other evidence on the ability of the economy to adjust to greater competition relates to the *structure of ownership* and *production*; the evidence is mixed. At present the industrial structure is not very concentrated and Slovenia produces some high tech goods, which together suggest that adjustment could be quite smooth. In addition, the number of private and smaller firms has increased. However, production and employment are still dominated by enterprises where management practices have not changed. A large proportion of medium-sized firms are owned by the management and workers, whose incentives to restructure, in particular through changes in working practices, are weak. In addition, in such enterprises, access to new capital and technology, which could facilitate restructuring, is relatively limited compared to foreign-owned firms. State-owned enterprises still represent an important part of production. The lack of effective monitoring and control structures on these enterprises is not beneficial for their restructuring.

Investment is relatively low as a percentage of GDP and to date has largely been in infrastructure (telecommunications and transport links) and the energy sector. A significant proportion has gone to 'non-productive' assets (e.g., land, buildings). This has understandably not produced immediate improvements in productivity performance, however it lays the basis for future gains. Although basic scientific research is at a high level, there is not enough investment in enterprise-based and applied research. At present the private sector accounts for only around 25 % of investment. The amount of *foreign direct investment* in Slovenia is also generally low, compared to the size of the economy. This is likely to be acting as a brake on restructuring, especially given that the firms with foreign investment are the most successful in terms of exports, returns on equity, and labour costs. The links between enterprises and their banks are often strong so that the latter find it hard to exert sufficient financial discipline on the former.

Agriculture is dominated by small dispersed individual farms. Technology, productivity and efficiency are all low, so there is still a significant need for adjustment, which could lead to lower employment in the sector.

The authorities are aware that the *legal system* still needs to be adapted further, and EU standards need to be adopted if Slovenia is to cope with competition within the Union. This will require a substantial input from the public administration, which needs to be strengthened in terms of coordination and implementation. In addition, the authorities have identified the need to clearly separate the legislative and executive branches of power to give Government a clearer role and facilitate policy implementation.

Although the *banking sector* is relatively well-developed, it is not competitive: operating costs are high, and there is a lack of competition in setting interest rates because of a cartel agreement. Because the number of banks is too high for the size and the economic needs of the country, the sector will need to consolidate.

The Slovenian authorities are devoting considerable resources to developing a consistent *medium-term macro- and microeconomic framework*, within which the necessary economic reforms to prepare for EU membership can be identified more easily and executed more smoothly.

Prospects and Priorities

The Slovenian authorities have adopted two medium term strategies: one for economic policy as a whole, and one for international policy specifically. The problems facing the economy have been clearly identified in the Governments medium-term strategy, but this has yet to be implemented. The focus for policy has shifted from macroeconomic stabilisation to microeconomic and structural adjustment. The aim is to boost competitiveness and revitalize the economy. The details of policy — e.g., financing, timing are being worked out.

Slovenia's strengths and weaknesses stem largely from the fact it is a small open economy which is relatively wealthy, and which has a strong consensual culture.

Slovenia has made substantial progress in achieving macroeconomic stability: inflation is in single digits, the budget deficit is low, the currency is stable and growth resumed in 1993. Progress on structural reform, on the other hand, has been much less rapid. The system lacks some dynamism, and has a weak record on restructuring and investment. As a result of this, growth remains relatively low, while inflationary pressures persist. Expansion is likely to be hampered to some extent in the short term by

the need to reform public finances further. For growth to begin accelerating again, competitiveness and export performance need to improve.

Progress in structural change has been relatively slow because the call for reform was less strong than elsewhere. Firstly, the economy was relatively wealthy, and still is. Secondly, the industrial decline after independence was less severe than elsewhere. Restructuring has been limited in part because of the method and speed of privatisation, which did not bring in new capital or new management. This helps explain why investment in technology and research and development at the enterprise level have been limited. Another factor is the high interest rates which discourage investment.

Inflationary pressure is strong. The necessary further liberalisation of prices for some key commodities will continue to put upward pressure on the price level. Additionally, inflation is fuelled by the indexation of wages and interest rates. To control inflation the degree of indexation needs to be reduced.

Competitiveness has been affected by the lack of investment in modern technology, the lack of restructuring and rising unit labour costs. The chosen method of privatisation, which favours incumbent managers and workers, does not encourage foreign investor participation or bring in much new capital. In many cases, it has not even resulted in substantially new work practices or restructuring. Domestic investment has been stronger in the social sector than in private sector, where it has been relatively limited because of high real interest rates and poor access to loans. As regards wages, the Social Agreements of 1994-1996 did go some way to steadying rises but only had limited success — real wage growth continued above productivity growth and above the targets set by the agreements. The need to contain wage growth is increasing but there has been no concerted attempt to deal with the main problem of indexation in the system. The Government has reduced non-wage labour costs, but they remain very high and budgetary constraints may make further reductions more difficult.

Slovenia still has to reform part of its public finances. At present the burden of social security contributions on labour is disproportionate and there is no VAT. Both of these issues will need to be addressed. VAT is now due to be introduced in 1999, which is considerably later than originally scheduled. The other challenge is to reform the pension and unemployment funds. Until recently these were self-financing. However, because of lower social contribution rates and demographic changes, which are going to worsen rather than improve, they have gone into deficit. To date the state budget has financed the deficit but there is a limit to how long this can go on.

Public administration has been reformed to a significant extent; however, the authorities still rightly feel the need to improve policy-making and implementation. At present there is a lack of co-ordination in those areas of policy where more than one ministry is involved.

2.3. General Evaluation

Slovenia can be regarded as a functioning market economy. It has advanced considerably in liberalisation and privatisation, and achieved a successful stabilisation of the economy. How-ever, there is a lack of competition in some sectors, in particular the financial sector, the working of the market mechanisms still needs some improvement, and the necessary reforms of the fiscal and social security systems are not yet completed.

Slovenia should be able to cope with competitive pressure and market forces within the Union in the medium term, provided that rigidities in the economy are reduced. It has a diverse export base, the workforce is skilled and highly trained, and infrastructure is relatively good. However, enterprise restructuring has been slow due to the consensual character of economic decision-making, and the incentives of workers and managers to preserve the status quo. Improvements in competitiveness have been hampered by rapid wage growth combined with low productivity growth. The low level of foreign direct investment reflects these structural problems, which need to be tackled.

3. Ability to Assume the Obligations of Membership

The European Council in Copenhagen included among the criteria for accession 'the ability to take on the obligations of membership, including adherence to the aims of political, economic and monetary union'.

In applying for membership on the basis of the Treaty, Slovenia has accepted without reserve the basic aims of the Union, including its policies and instruments. This chapter examines Slovenia's capacity to assume the obligations of membership — that is, the legal and institutional framework, known as the *acquis*, by means of which the Union puts into effect its objectives.

With the development of the Union, the *acquis* has become progressively more onerous, and presents a greater challenge for future accessions than was the case in the past. The ability of Slovenia to implement the *acquis* will be central to its capacity to function successfully within the Union.

The following sections examine, for each main field of the Union's activity, the current and prospective situation of Slovenia. The starting-point of the description and analysis is a brief summary of the *acquis*, with a mention of the provisions of the Europe Agreement and the White Paper, where they are relevant. Finally, for each field of activity there is a brief assessment of Slovenia's ability to assume the obligations of membership on a medium-term horizon.

3.1. Internal Market without Frontiers

Article 7a of the Treaty defines the Union's internal market as an area without internal frontiers in which the free movement of goods, persons, services and capital is ensured. This internal market, central to the integration process, is based on an open-market economy in which competition and economic and social cohesion must play a full part.

Effective implementation of the liberties enshrined in the Treaty requires not only compliance with such important principles as, for example, non-discrimination or mutual recognition of national regulations — as clarified by Court of Justice rulings — but also concomitant, effective application of a series of common specific provisions. These are designed, in particular, to provide safety, public health, environmental and consumer protection, public confidence in the services sector, appropriately qualified persons to practise certain specialist occupations and, where necessary, introduction or coordination of regulatory and monitoring mechanisms; all systematic checks and inspections necessary to ensure correct application of the rules are carried out on the market, not at frontier crossings.

It is important to incorporate Community legislation into national legislation effectively, but even more important to implement it properly in the field, via the appropriate administrative and judicial structures set up in the Member States and respected by companies. This is an essential precondition for creating the mutual trust indispensable for smooth operation of the internal market.

This chapter must be read in conjunction with, *inter alia*, the chapters on social policy, the environment, consumer protection and sectoral policies.

The Four Freedoms

A step-by-step approach is being taken to absorption of the *acquis* by the candidate countries:

☐ the Association Agreement between the Community, its Member States and Slovenia was signed in 1996 and is being ratified. With regard to the four freedoms and approximation of legislation, the Agreement provides, in particular, for immediate or gradual application of a number of obligations, some of them reciprocal, covering, in particular, freedom of establishment, national treatment, free trade, intellectual property and public procurement;

☐ preceding the entry into effect of the Europe Agreement, the Interim Agreement provides for the implementation of the trade and trade-related aspects as stipulated under the Europe Agreement with effect from 1 January 1997;

☐ the Commission's 1995 White Paper (COM (95) 163 final), guidelines, intended to help the candidate countries prepare for integration into the internal market, gives a closer definition of the legislation concerned. It identifies the 'key measures' with a direct effect on the free movement of goods, services, capital and persons and outlines the conditions necessary in order to operate the legislation, including the legal and organisational structures. Twenty-three areas of Community activity are examined, dividing the measures into two stages, in order of priority, to provide a work programme for the pre-accession phase. The Technical Assistance and Information Exchange Office (TAIEX) was set up with the objective of providing complementary and focused technical assistance in the areas of legislation covered in the White Paper. A legislative database has recently been established by the Office;

☐ the candidate countries will have to transpose and implement all the *acquis*. The 'Action Plan for the Single Market' submitted to the Amsterdam European Council gives details of the priority measures necessary to make the Single Market work better between the Fifteen in preparation for introduction of the single currency. This will inevitably entail changes to the *acquis*.

General Framework

Whatever their field of activity, undertakings must be able to operate on the basis of common rules. These are important since they shape the general framework within which economies operate and, hence, the general conditions of competition. They include the rules on competition (on undertakings and state aid) and tax measures discussed elsewhere in this Opinion, the opening-up of public works, supply and service contracts, harmonisation of the rules on intellectual property (including the European patent), harmonisation of the rules on company law and accountancy, protection of personal data, transfer of proceedings and recognition of judgments (Article 220 Conventions).

Descriptive Summary

Public procurement is regulated by a 1997 framework law, which is intended to implement part of the EC requirements as a first step. Implementing decrees are in the process of being adopted by the Government. A Public Procurement Unit under the Ministry of Finance is in charge of monitoring the public procurement system, preparing new legislation and issuing instructions. According to this law an independent Audit Committee will be appointed by Parliament to rule on all requests for audit of decisions.

Based on the Law on Industrial Property (1992/1993) and on the Law on Intellectual Property (1992/1993), *intellectual* and *industrial property* legislation in Slovenia is well developed. The Intellectual Property Office is in charge of monitoring legislation in the intellectual and industrial property field and coordinating enforcement in cooperation with customs, police and the Trade Inspectorate. The TRIPS Agreement is applicable to Slovenia.

Company law is governed by the 1993 Law on Commercial Companies. Currently, 48 000 companies of various types are registered. Companies can issue shares to raise finance, and shareholders are protected in this event. Minimum capital requirements are laid down by law. There are safeguard clauses for the protection of authorised capital. Different obligations exist for the protection of creditors depending on the type of company. Companies are required to publicise information about major decisions affecting them. There is a register of companies in which all the essential information regarding each company is kept. Articles 246(5) and 449(6) of the Law on Commercial Companies stipulate that the majority of directors of joint stock and limited liability companies have to be citizens of Slovenia. There are also provisions restricting the operation of foreign firms in Slovenia through branches, thereby limiting the freedom of establishment (Articles 561 to 568).

The *accounting* field is regulated by Chapter 7 of the Law on Commercial Companies (1993). There is a Law on Audit (1993). The Slovenian Institute of Auditors is authorised to adopt accounting standards and to issue certificates to auditors.

Article 38 of the Slovenian Constitution provides for the *protection of personal data*. Based on that article, the law of 7 March 1990 establishes the institutional framework for the protection of data, including a supervisory authority. Slovenia acceded in May 1994 to the Council of Europe Convention No 108 on data protection.

Current and Prospective Assessment

The new Slovene legislation on *public procurement* only incorporates part of the scope of the EC directives. Rules on selection and award criteria will need to be clarified. The system of legal remedies is not fully compatible with the EC requirements. Furthermore, utilities sectors do not seem to be covered.

At present, Slovene firms (including Slovene subsidiaries of EU firms) obtain preferential treatment as regards the award of public procurement contracts. This system of preferences could be maintained only up to the end of the transition period allowed by the Europe Agreement (i.e. 6 years after entry into force). Complete harmonisation in the field of public procurement is expected to be achieved by the end of 1999. Slovenia's authorities recognise that changes to the draft law will most certainly be needed to meet EC requirements.

Intellectual and *industrial property* legislation is with minor exceptions compatible with the *acquis communautaire*. Aspects remaining to be harmonised include the duration of the protection of audio-visual productions and the introduction of Supplementary Protection Certificates. As regards the implementation of legislation, in particular in the pharmaceutical sector, the exhaustion of trade marks still needs to be addressed.

It is further intended to address provisional measures and the preservation of evidence in infringement procedures and border measures by amending existing legislation in 1999. In practice, the administrative structures are not fully equipped, especially as regards their staffing levels and training, to enforce legislation adequately.

According to the information on *company law* provided by Slovenia, its legislation is already in line with the First, Third, Eleventh and Twelfth Directives, and it is understood that the one remaining derogation from the Second Directive and also the restrictions against foreign directors and foreign firms are likely to be abolished in 1997.

With regard to *accounting*, nearly all requirements in the Fouth, Seventh and Eighth Directives appear to have been implemented. One change in the Law on Audit is planned, to allow an audit to be conducted by a self-employed auditor, not only by an auditing firm. Certain transitional problems are in evidence relating to the implementation in practice of the new rules, including a shortage of qualified accountants and auditors, but these can be solved in the medium term.

The accession of Slovenia to Council of Europe Convention No 108 indicates that Slovenian legislation on *data protection* is in line with European standards as laid down in that Convention. Moreover, an authority competent to supervise the implementation of the legislation has already been established, the powers of which are clearly laid down in the law. Nevertheless, Slovene legislation is not yet fully in line with the EC framework Directive. A new law is expected. Implementation and enforcement also need to be strengthened.

In the field of *civil law* it should be noted that the Convention of Lugano on jurisdiction and the enforcement of decisions in civil and commercial matters is not, for the time being, open to Slovenia, which needs to make progress in the area of protection of civil interests, subject to the assessment of the States already party to the Convention.

Conclusion

Slovenia has already largely taken on the most important directives in the sectors indicated above. Implementation of the provisions of the Europe Agreement and the White Paper's recommendations covering the sectors reviewed has generally been good.

However, further work is required in the area of public procurement, where Slovenia will need to make comprehensive amendments to its recently introduced legislation in order to reach full alignment with the corresponding EC directives. Regarding intellectual property, there is scope for further strengthening implementation procedures and enforcement of legislation. In the fields of company law and accounting, no problems are foreseen, assuming the legislative

timetable proceeds as planned, including the repeal of the discriminatory provisions in company law referred to above. In the field of data protection, further efforts are required to bring legislation fully into line with the EC framework Directive. Implementation and enforcement capacities need to be strengthened. This should be possible in the medium term.

Free Movement of Goods

Free movement of goods can be achieved only by removing measures which restrict trade — not only customs duties and quantitative restrictions but all measures with equivalent, i.e. protectionist, effect, irrespective of whether or not they are specifically aimed at domestic or imported products. Where technical standards are not harmonised, the free movement of goods must be ensured by applying the principle of mutual recognition of national rules and accepting the rule that national specifications should be no more stringent than is required to achieve their legitimate objectives. This rule was established in the *Cassis de Dijon* judgment.

For the purpose of harmonisation, the European Community has developed the 'New Approach' which introduces an approach carefully balanced between Government and private autonomous bodies and in which European Community legislation and European standards play a distinct complementary role. Thus, instead of imposing technical solutions, European Community legislation is limited to establishing the essential requirements which products must meet. Products manufactured in accordance with European standards are presumed to meet such essential requirements, but European standards are not the only way to prove such conformity. The 'New Approach' works in conjunction with the 'Global Approach' on product certification which governs the apposition of the 'CE Mark' on the product. For other products such as pharmaceuticals, chemicals, motor vehicles, and food products, European Community directives follow the traditional regulatory pattern of providing fully detailed rules.

The free movement of goods also dictates that a number of Community harmonisation measures be transposed into national law. Implementation of health and safety harmonisation rules is particularly important and requires the establishment of appropriate mechanisms and organisations, both for businesses and the authorities.

Two of the 'horizontal' directives essential to smooth running of the Single Market are the Directive on general product safety and the Directive on liability for defective products. The regulations concerning general product safety are covered in the section on consumer protection.

The rules on agricultural products (compliance with veterinary and plant-health standards) are explained in detail in the section on agriculture.

Descriptive Summary

Slovenia started on its path towards establishing the conditions for the free movement of goods with the entry into force of the Interim Agreement on 1 January 1997.

All prices have been liberalised, with the exceptions of those for public utilities, foodstuffs and agricultural prices.

With regard to technical barriers to trade, the process of alignment is proceeding rather slowly. In some areas federal regulations of the former SFRY are still being used as national regulations in Slovenia.

Concerning legislative alignment, Slovenia has made some progress, following a period of standstill in the second half of 1996. However, the legislative approximation programme presented in May 1997 is rather weak both in scope and substance of legislative alignment.

The Slovene Standards and Metrology Institute (SMIS), a government-linked body, is entrusted with both the standardisation and accreditation functions, this latter traditionally belonging to the public sphere.

Overall, the standardisation activity is progressing well. By June 1997, SMIS, which is an affiliate member of the Comité européen de normalisation (CEN) and the Comité européen de normalisation électrotechnique (Cenelec), had issued more than 1 200 standards, the great majority of which transpose either European or international Organisation for Standards/International Electrotechnical Commission (ISO/CEI) standards. However, there is still a considerable stock of former Yugoslav regulations in force of mandatory application, many of which require different forms of mandatory third-party certification.

Current and Prospective Assessment

Slovenia has been liberalising progressively its trade regime. Nonetheless, further efforts are required for the full adoption and implementation of the *acquis*.

There remain a number of restrictive measures relating to foreign trade, including the regime of import licensing. About 3 % of imports require special government licenses or are subject to quantitative restrictions. The new set of pan-European rules of origin, applied by Slovenia from 1 January 1997, will further favour trade and free circulation.

In some cases Slovene mandatory standards and certification requirements create technical barriers to trade. Additional removal of technical barriers to trade will be achieved once Slovenia has adopted EU technical legislation and taken over EU concepts.

Legislative alignment has just started in early 1997, after some period of standstill. The legislative approximation programme presented in May 1997 covers considerable ground but is rather weak both in scope and substance of legislative alignment. New Approach directives are not mentioned and approximation is unclear in the chemicals and foodstuffs sector. In some areas, however, legislative alignment seems to be progressing satisfactorily, such as on pharmaceuticals and the automotive sector. The late adoption of the Law on Standards, being envisaged for 1999, will affect progress in negotiations on the European Conformity Assessment Agreement.

According to the Slovene authorities major legislative measures should be transposed by the year 2000. It needs to be borne in mind, in any case, that secondary legislation is often necessary to implement the general legislative framework. However, the limited endowment of human resources and technical expertise of Slovenia may hinder a smooth approximation process and the setting up of relevant implementation structures, thereby making the reform process difficult.

In addition, adequate structures and staffing for market surveillance should be established and developed in the competent public authorities for the ex-post control of product safety. With regard to the necessary structures to apply the *acquis*, Slovenia has yet to achieve the required separation between the regulatory, standardisation and product certification functions, for the latter two of which more emphasis should be put on the involvement of the private sector.

The current Slovene legislation concerning civil liability for defective products does not yet conform fully to the EC requirements in that area. However, amendments are already planned in this respect.

In the areas subject to national rules and not covered by Community harmonisation, there is not enough information available to assess whether Community legal principles on the free movement of goods are properly applied in Slovenia. The reporting procedures which form part of the internal-market machinery are not yet operational and so cannot be used in the pre-accession period. The most important instruments in this connection are: Directive 83/189/EEC, requiring governments to report draft national technical standards and regulations; Decision No 3052/95/EC on measures derogating from the principle of the free movement of goods; procedures by which complaints can be submitted to the Commission; and Article 177 of the Treaty, enabling Member States to ask for preliminary rulings from the Court of Justice. It is also hard to assess whether Slovenia complies with the principle of mutual recognition; more information is required on its national rules, and on administrative practices, which can have an effect on product sales.

Conclusion

While limited progress has been made towards adopting the *acquis* related to the free movement of goods, considerable further work is needed. In this respect, the implementation of the provisions of the Interim and Europe Agreement will contribute to progress over the next years.

Efforts will have to be strengthened to align technical legislation, including New Approach Directives. The standardisation and conformity assessment system also needs to be strengthened. A speedy adoption of the new Law on Standards would help in this respect. Human resources, skill and institution building should be equally upgraded. Provided current efforts are increased, free circulation of goods could be completed in

the medium term. The Slovenian authorities should also see to it — in the fields not covered by Community harmonisation — that their national law is not likely to hinder trade, notably by ensuring that the measures in force are proportional to the objectives pursued.

Free Movement of Capital

The Europe Agreement establishes the principle of the free movement of capital between Slovenia and the EU. This applies from the entry into force of the Europe Agreement as regards direct investments made by companies already established in Slovenia and as regards branches and agencies of Community companies (as well as the self-employed), gradually during the transitional period.

It also prohibits the introduction of any new foreign exchange restriction from its entry into force.

The White Paper highlights the link between the free movement of capital and the free movement of financial services. It suggests a sequence of capital liberalisation starting from long-term capital movements and those linked to commercial transactions to short-term capital.

Descriptive Summary

Between 1990-1996 foreign direct investment (FDI) reached 600 million ECU. By the end of 1996, the share of FDI in GDP was 10,8 %. Taking into consideration the level of GDP in Slovenia, FDI is moderate. The small size of the market explains part of it. However, there are also restrictions to FDI. These refer mainly to the way the privatisation of socially-owned enterprises has been implemented (mainly through management buy outs accompanied by restrictive stipulations for portfolio investments by foreigners), to overall tightened controls on foreign capital inflows and to various sector specific restrictions.

Both the Government and the private sector have access to the international financial markets. However, interest-free deposits in tolar for non-government borrowers have been increased to 40 % for loans with a maturity up to seven years (and 10 % for longer-term loans). Other measures taken by the Bank of Slovenia comprise the introduction of custody accounts for foreign investors, increases in obligatory bank reserves for foreign loans and ceilings for remittances from residents' accounts.

In September 1995 Slovenia officially accepted the obligations of Article VIII of the IMF and thus formally established full current account convertibility of the tolar. Current account transactions had been, in practice, freed a few years before.

Capital outflow is, in general, subject to authorisation while the regime applicable to capital has been recently restricted as well. Among the liberalised capital movements are foreign direct investment in the country (with exceptions) and abroad (under certain conditions), commercial credits, personal capital movements (except loan operations) and financial credits and loans (with exceptions/limitations).

Current and Prospective Assessment

A notable characteristic of the legal framework concerning capital movements is that no provisions exist for the implementation of operations in securities. This implies that, concerning the purchase, sale or other operations in securities, the provisions governing direct investment, or borrowing and lending, apply by analogy.

In order to establish the legal basis for the further liberalisation of capital transactions and to cover grey areas of existing legislation, notably for operations in securities, a new Law on Foreign Exchange is scheduled to be adopted early 1998.

The prohibition against establishment of branches and cross border provision of services by EU investment is intended to be removed with the introduction of the Foreign Exchange Act early 1998. Effective legislation needs to be put in place for the management of pension funds.

The approximation of legislation as regards the capital market corresponds, in general, to the obligations undertaken in the Europe Agreement. However, some decrees adopted by the Bank of Slovenia are not in line with the Agreement. The following specific issues deserve further attention:

a) the issue of the acquisition of real estate by non-residents in Slovenia;

b) according to provisions in Slovenia's company legislation, the majority of members of companies' boards of directors must be Slovenian nationals. This provision is restrictive and provides a disincentive for the acquisition by non-residents of controlling stakes in Slovene companies. The Government is aware of the problem and intends to remove the provisions as far as banks and insurance companies are concerned through the new banking and insurance laws. At present, however, no change in these provisions is foreseen for the other sectors;

c) high interest-free deposits in tolar for non-government borrowers constitute an important restriction on the free movement of capital;

d) tight registration procedures, based on the compulsory establishment of custody accounts, and high transaction costs, due to high foreign currency reserves to be built up by the banks have a negative effect on foreign investment and loans.

The scope and the justification of the measures adopted by the Bank of Slovenia will have to be examined in further detail. Overall, the restrictions introduced early 1997 tighten further the control over foreign exchange transactions, have a negative effect on foreign investments and loans, and should be phased out.

Conclusion

Overall, liberalisation of capital movements is slow. Despite substantial progress in the approximation of legislation, reflecting the stipulations of both the White Paper and the Europe Agreement, recent measures adopted by the Bank of Slovenia caused a set back to the liberalisation efforts.

The Government is aware of these problems and has the intention to introduce some capital liberalisation measures, including the possibility of foreign banks to open branches in Slovenia, through a new Foreign Exchange Act. However, under the current framework of monetary and exchange policies, there is little prospect of an important move towards further capital liberalisation. Therefore macroeconomic foreign direct investment policies should be reviewed in order to be compatible with more liberal movements and to promote higher foreign direct investment.

Free Movement of Services

The basis of the free movement of services is the prohibition of discrimination, in particular on grounds of nationality, and rules on the alignment of divergent national legislation. These rules often concern both the right of establishment, which comes under the heading of the free movement of persons, and the freedom to provide services. Their implementation implies the establishment of administrative structures (banking control boards, audio-visual control authorities, regulatory bodies) and greater cooperation between Member States in the area of enforcement (mutual recognition arrangements).

A substantial amount of the legislation applicable to the free movement of services relates to financial services. It also concerns the problems relating to the opening-up of national markets in the sectors traditionally dominated by monopolies, e.g. telecommunications and, to a certain extent, energy and transport. These subjects will be dealt with in the sections of the Opinion specifically referring to them.

Descriptive Summary

With three important exceptions all *banks* are currently privately owned. There are no branches of foreign banks allowed. The balance sheet total has been growing steadily, both in absolute terms and as a percentage of GDP. The three biggest banks cover more than half of the market.

The 1991 Law on Banks and Saving Institutions regulates the establishment, operation and supervision of banks and savings institutions. Because of the underdeveloped financial system the law also includes some provisions which enabled the domestic banking system to adjust to the international financial environment.

Supervision of banks and savings banks is performed by the Bank Supervision Department of the Central Bank. A comprehensive system of banking laws and regulations is in place and the Central Bank monitors closely its implementation.

The problem of poor asset quality has been addressed after the promulgation by the Bank of decrees setting out rules and regulations on calculating provisions as security against potential losses. Foreign banks may establish subsidiaries in Slovenia, which benefit from national treatment, or a representative office. They cannot open branches, but the abolition of these restrictions is foreseen under the new banking legislation discussed in Parliament.

All banks meet the 8 % international capital adequacy requirement and in fact exceed it considerably. To operate with a full-license a bank must have at a minimum 4 080 million SIT or about 25 million ECU at the end-1996 exchange rate and must also be active in retail banking in Slovenia.

A new Banking Law is scheduled to be adopted by end 1997. Besides the Basel Standards, all relevant EU Directives are taken into account. This law targets particularly at adjusting the Slovene banking sector to international criteria and standards.

There is only one regulated market, namely the Ljubljana *stock exchange*, access to which is also allowed to credit institutions. The Exchange is a self-regulatory organisation whose responsibilities include the adoption of provisions concerning access to the market, listing requirements, real-time disclosure of market information via radio broadcasting and data reporting to the authority. The Ljubljana Stock Exchange is member of the International Organisation of Securities Commissions (IOSCO) and the emerging markets committee. Foreign ownership of brokerage is limited to 24 % of their capital.

The securities market is regulated by the 1994 Law on the Securities Market and, for the establishment and the operation of investment companies and mutual funds, the 1994 Law on Investment Funds and Managing Companies. The regulation of the market was modelled after the US Securities and Exchange Commission. The regulation and supervision of the securities market is performed by the independent Securities and Exchange Agency. There is a centralised securities register, the 'central register of dematerialised securities'.

Five *insurance* companies have a social ownership (public but not State), in two of them the social ownership exceeds 50 %. The biggest insurance company covers 56 % of the market and has 80 % of total own funds. There is one state-controlled export credit insurer.

The legal framework for insurance companies is the Insurance Companies Act, published in 1994 and 1995. The regulation and supervision of the market is currently being implemented while further measures are envisaged. The 1994 Insurance Companies Act authorises, upon approval of the Insurance Supervisory Authority, foreign establishments only through participations of up to 15 % of the capital. Foreign investors can buy additional shares in Slovene insurance companies subject to approval by the Supervisory Authority. The legal basis for the establishment of the Insurance Supervision Authority is set by the above Insurance Companies Act.

Since 1995, the activities of the supervisory authority have been carried out by the Insurance Supervisory Authority, a body part of the Ministry of Finance.

Recapitalisation of the insurance sector is expected to take until 1999. Investment abroad is not allowed. In the case of re-insurance, there is limited access to the local market.

Current and Prospective Assessment

In the *banking sector*, laws and regulations adopted after Slovenia's independence are similar to those of the EU, namely to the Stage I measures, and are being further harmonised with European directives under the new legislation to be adopted by the end of 1997. This will contribute further to the increase in efficiency of the banking system as it becomes part of the European and global banking sector.

The recent introduction of custody accounts for foreign investors in Slovenia, linked with a restrictive licensing and foreign currency reserve policy, limits the number of banks entitled to carry out foreign capital transactions, excluding also the foreign banks which do not provide retail services in Slovenia, because these are not eligible to a full license. Only a full licence grants a bank the right to open custody accounts and thus perform the above transactions.

Approximation to White Paper Stage I measures was achieved by the adoption of the *Securities Market* Law, 1994. The Agency for the Securities Market lacks the power to perform its supervision duties efficiently. The transposition of the principles laid down by the Investment Services and Capital Adequacy Directives is currently under scrutiny by the Government.

Credit institutions, which may be authorised by the Bank of Slovenia (with prior opinion of the securities supervisor) to provide investment ser-

vices, cannot have more than one stockbroking firm as a subsidiary. Establishment of branches and cross-border provision of services from third countries is not allowed. A 24 % ceiling is imposed on non-residents' stake in stockbroking firms. However, EU investment firms may hold majority interests in local credit institutions authorised by the Bank of Slovenia to provide investment services.

The prohibition against establishment of branches and cross-border provision of services by EU investment firms is intended to be removed with the introduction of the Foreign Exchange Act early 1998.

In the field of insurance Slovene legislation still has to undergo some adjustments to EU legislation as regards the supervisory system, provisions for foreign investments and the lack of transparency in the application of regulations. Problems remain to be solved concerning privatisation. Restrictions on setting up branches in Slovenia need to be removed.

Supervision of the sector is still in the early stages of its development. The Insurance Supervisory Authority was installed in March 1996 within the Ministry of Finance but needs further strengthening.

Conclusion

Substantial progress has been achieved. The *acquis* in this sector has already been to a considerable extent transposed, but important provisions still remain to be adopted. Full free establishment in the areas of banking, securities and insurance, in particular with regard to branches of foreign institutions, still has to be adequately introduced in the sectors' legislative frameworks and duly implemented.

Foreign banks are currently excluded in practice from foreign capital transactions, as these are reserved to banks benefiting from a full licence, whose grant is subject to a very high capital flow and to the provision of a full range of services in Slovenia (including retail services).

As regards insurance, privatisation should be speeded up and the insurance and reinsurance sector opened up to EU operators and to foreign investment. The supervisory functions in the sector are expected to be strengthened by the new legislation under preparation.

However, provided harmonisation proceeds as planned, no major difficulties are foreseen in achieving full approximation in relation to free movement of financial services in the medium term.

Free Movement of Persons

The free movement of persons encompasses two concepts with different logical implications in the Treaty. On the one hand, Article 7a in Part One of the Treaty on 'Principles' mentions the concept in connection with the establishment of the internal market and implies that persons are not to be subject to controls when crossing the internal frontiers between the Member States. On the other hand, Article 8a in Part Two of the Treaty on 'Citizenship of the Union' gives every citizen of the Union the individual right to move and reside freely within the territory of the Member States, subject to certain conditions. The abolition of frontier checks must apply to all persons, whatever their nationality, if Article 7a is not to be meaningless. While the rights deriving from Article 8a apply in all Member States, those stemming from Article 7a have not yet been fully applied throughout the Union.

a) Free Movement of Union Citizens, Freedom of Establishment and Mutual Recognition of Diplomas and Qualifications

The Europe Agreement provides for the non-discriminatory treatment of workers that are legally employed (as well as their families). It covers the possibility of cumulating or transferring social security rights, and encourages Member States to conclude bilateral agreements with Slovenia on access to labour markets. During the second phase of the transitional period, the Association Council will examine further ways of improving the movement of workers.

The White Paper considers the legislative requirements in order to achieve a harmonious development of the labour market, whilst simultaneously preventing distortions of competition.

The free movement of workers is one of the fundamental freedoms enshrined in the Treaty; freedom to practise certain professions (e.g. in the legal and health fields) may, however, be subject to certain conditions, such as qualifications. Depending on the case, these may be dealt with through coordination or by applying the principle of mutual recognition. Freedom of establishment is also guaranteed under the Treaty and covers the economic activity of self-employed natural persons and companies.

The free choice of place of residence may thus be subject to minimum conditions as to resources and health insurance where the person does not exercise a profession in the country concerned.

Descriptive Summary

According to current legislation, foreigners are basically entitled with equal rights as regards working conditions as well as in the field of social security with certain exceptions linked to the status of permanent residence.

The issue of a work permit is conditioned upon the non-availability in the area of prospective employment of a suitable local worker. Work permits are normally issued for only one year and only for work with a single employer. In case, the worker loses the employment he must leave the country. Family members of foreign workers do not acquire the right to work. There is scope for the State to develop further initiatives aimed at economic and social integration of foreigners. However, Slovenia is currently preparing new immigration legislation following European standards and principles which will address these issues.

Concerning training, major efforts have been undertaken by the Slovene Government to conform with EU Directives. Slovenia has largely taken up the *acquis*. Structures (ministries and public bodies) are in place for many professions, but these need to be reinforced.

Current and Prospective Assessment

Slovenia has made significant efforts to adapt its social legislation to EU standards. With minor exceptions, Slovene legislation already recognises the principle of non-discrimination between nationals and foreigners legally residing in the country. Therefore, the application of the principle of equal treatment to those EU workers already legally residing in Slovenia should not be a problem.

Current restrictions on the employment of non-national employees in top managerial positions are to be abolished with the new Company legislation scheduled to be adopted by the end of 1997.

Most of the *acquis* concerning the mutual recognition of diplomas and qualifications have already been taken on board. However, there are still important areas where continued efforts are required. Full approximation is to be achieved in the medium term.

Training, where coordinated by directives for seven professions, is broadly in line with the *acquis* although some adaptation is still necessary. Professional structures (such as professional chambers or associations) are in place for many professions but these will probably need to be reinforced in the future. Integration with EU professional associations is developing well (for example, engineering diplomas already meet the minimum European standards).

Conclusion

Policies on immigration and work permits are handled restrictively, but legal amendments are under preparation. On mutual recognition of diplomas, some areas remain to be adjusted.

Slovenia is aware of the outstanding issues that need to be resolved with regard to the free movement of persons. From a technical point of view, adaptations of regulations will be necessary in the medium term.

b) Abolition of Checks on Persons at Internal Frontiers

The free movement of persons within the meaning of Article 7a of the EC Treaty, i.e. the abolition of checks on all persons, whatever their nationality, at the internal frontiers has not yet been fully implemented in the Union. Doing away with checks on persons is conditional on the introduction of a large number of accompanying measures, some of which have yet to be approved and implemented by the Member States (see separate section on Justice and Home Affairs). However, that objective has been achieved by a limited number of Member States in accordance with the Schengen Convention (seven Member States already apply it and

another six are working towards implementation).

The draft Treaty aims to make that objective easier to achieve within the Union by including a new chapter on Freedom, Security and Justice and incorporating the Schengen Agreement into the EU.

Slovenia has stated its desire and readiness to fulfil the provisions of the Schengen *acquis*. It has begun preparations to this end and has sought assistance in this connection from Member States, notably in regard to the strengthening of borders controls. Amendments necessary to the Border Control Act and the Law on Foreigners are already part of the three-year legislative programme of the Government.

General Evaluation

Slovenia's progress in the implementation of legislation relating to the White Paper is summarised in the Annex. According to the table, Slovenia considers that by 30 June 1997 it will have adopted national implementing legislation for 415 of the 899 directives and regulations in the White Paper. That figure covers provisions for which Slovenia considers it will have adopted implementing legislation or which it will have checked for compatibility with Community rules and does not prejudge actual compatibility as such, on which the Commission is not able at this stage to state an opinion.

As regards all the fields relating to the internal market, and in particular the fields of accountancy, mutual recognition of professional qualifications and intellectual property, the Community legislative basis is practically in place. Legislation has been adopted in full or in part to implement most of the measures, according to the Slovenian authorities' assessment, though the Commission cannot at this stage express a position on its total compatibility with Community law. Slovenia still has to make a considerable legislative effort to achieve full conformity with the *acquis*. It is also necessary to strengthen the coordination and implementation of the national strategy for approximation of legislation.

Despite the progress already achieved, the genuine progress already achieved in the transposition of the texts adopted in the very recent past must go hand in hand with concrete implementing measures and the creation of an effective administrative infrastructure. Substantial work is still however required in the areas of public procurement, insurance, freedom of capital movements, product conformity and standardisation, indirect taxation. Implementation and enforcement should be considered an integral part of the Slovene pre-accession strategy, which should go beyond primary legislation and also include technical standards.

As things currently stand, the Commission cannot yet express an opinion on the capacity of companies, particularly small and medium-sized businesses, to implement the *acquis*.

Leaving aside certain specific aspects relating to agriculture, checks at the internal frontiers of the Union can only be abolished once sufficient legislative harmonisation has been achieved. This calls for mutual confidence, based in particular on sound administration (e.g. the importance of safety checks on some products at the place of departure). As far as goods are concerned, the completion of the internal market on 1 January 1993 was only achieved by doing away with all the formalities and checks performed by the Member States at the internal borders of the Union.

In particular these checks covered particularly technical points (product safety), veterinary, animal-health and plant-health matters, economic and commercial matters (e.g. prevention of counterfeiting of goods), security (weapons, etc.) and environmental aspects (waste, etc.).

In most cases, the abolition of checks was only made possible by the adoption and application of Community measures harmonising the rules on movement and placement on the market (particularly as regards product safety) and, where applicable, by shifting the place where controls and formalities within the Member States or on their markets are conducted (in particular as regards VAT and excise duties, veterinary and plant-health checks, and the collection of statistics).

A section of Slovenia's present borders will become the Union's external frontier and this means border checks will need to be stepped up (see separate section on Customs).

In view of the overall assessment that can be made of progress achieved to date and the rate at which work is advancing in the various areas concerned, it is difficult at present to put a time-scale on Slovenia's ability to take over and implement all the instruments required to abolish internal border checks and to transfer those checks to the Union's external frontier.

Slovenia has already adopted significant elements of the *acquis* relating to the Single Market. However, the Commission is not yet able to take a position on every measure whose transposition has been reported by Slovenia. In any case, progress has been limited in some important sectors, notably the liberalisation of capital movements, indirect taxation and technical regulations and standards. In most areas, enforcement needs to be strengthened. Provided current efforts continue, or are stepped up in areas where progress is lagging, it can be expected that in the medium term Slovenia will have adopted and implemented the Single Market legislation and made the necessary progress on the mechanisms of enforcement in the medium term, in order to be able to participate fully in the internal market.

Competition

European Community competition policy derives from Article 3 (g) of the Treaty providing that the Community shall have a *system ensuring that competition in the internal market is not distorted*. The main areas of application are anti-trust and state aid.

The Europe Agreement provides for a competition regime to be applied in trade relations between the Community and Slovenia based on the criteria of Articles 85 and 86 of the EC Treaty (agreements between undertakings/abuses of dominant position) and in Article 92 (state aid) and for implementing rules in these fields to be adopted within three years of the entry into force of the Agreement.

Furthermore, it provides that Slovenia will make its legislation compatible with that of the Community in the field of competition.

The White Paper refers to the progressive application of the above provisions and those of the Merger Regulation [(EEC) No 4064/89] and of Articles 37 and 90 (Monopolies and Special Rights).

Descriptive Summary

Competition is currently regulated by the *Law on the Protection of Competition* (Official Gazette RS No 18/1993 dated April 9, 1993). The *Bureau for the Protection of Competition* is the single authority responsible for the implementation of the Act. It was officially established in October 1994 and is responsible to the Ministry of Economic Relations and Development.

In order to be in line with the current and foreseeable situation in the EU as regards *sectors subject to monopolies or dominant positions* such as telecommunications, transport, postal services and energy, necessary measures have either already been taken or are under preparation. On the basis of information available, no state monopoly of commercial character exists in Slovenia.

As regards *state aid* there is as yet no authority responsible for the monitoring of state aid, but the necessary legislation for the appointment of this authority and the monitoring of state aid in Slovenia is under preparation. No reliable aid inventory exists at present.

Current and Prospective Assessment

In order to be compatible with *EC competition rules*, a series of amendments to the Law on the Protection of Competition is required. This applies mainly to its scope of application (sectors like transport, storage, servicing are excluded from the application), the introduction of prohibition on restrictive agreements and the definition of dominant position and the abuse of dominance. Further clarification is required on joint venture and merger control procedures. Provisions dealing with investigation, business secrets and rights of defence are still to be developed. If adopted the new draft competition law will go a long way towards satisfying these concerns.

Apparently, Slovenia has started its policy of liberalising and opening up to competition certain traditional *sectors subject to monopolies* such as telecommunications and postal services. More information should be provided to give a viable evaluation of the situation in the other sectors.

State aid are not monitored and hence reliable information is not available yet. Establishing an inventory and setting up a monitoring authority should be a matter of priority. The aid inventory should cover all measures granted by the State, regional or local authorities or through State resources. The provision of sufficient staff and technical facilities to carry out a credible State aid control is equally crucial. While the abolition of the export aid measures is welcomed, certain measures constitute operating aids which are only allowed under very strict conditions. Due to the lack of transparency, it is unclear whether these conditions are complied with.

Considerable effort has been made within a rather short period of time to prepare an inventory on the existing aid. The Government has also started the drafting and adoption of the rules necessary to introduce state aid control and is in the process of appointing the monitoring authority.

In addition to the adoption of legislation sufficiently approximate to that of the EU, *credible enforcement* of competition law requires the establishment of well functioning anti-trust and state aid monitoring authorities. It requires moreover that the judicial system, the public administration and the relevant economic operators have a sufficient understanding of competition law and policy.

Conclusion

In respect of *anti-trust* the current level of approximation of legislation is not satisfactory. However, if the new draft law on competition is adopted the process of approximation will be close to completed. The Bureau for the Protection of Competition needs to be strengthened in order to ensure a credible enforcement of the law.

In the field of *state aid* the requirements as regards transparency and monitoring of state aid have not yet been fulfilled. It will require a substantial effort from Slovenia in order to meet these requirements in the medium term. Due to the present lack of experience in the field close cooperation with the Commission will be necessary in a foreseeable future.

It seems, moreover, that in certain sectors *exclusive* or *special rights* exist which may not be compatible with the Community *acquis*. These problems should be addressed in the near future.

3.2. Innovation

Information Society

Present Situation

The economic and social effects made possible by the combination of information technology and telecommunications are great. In Slovenia these possibilities were neglected before 1989 although education generally was not. The result seems to be that demand for computers has spurted beyond normal expectation deduced from GDP per capita. The existence of host computers on the Internet (7,4 per 1 000 inhabitants) as a relative measure of development towards the Information Society IS suggests that Slovenia has reached today the EC average. If Internet connections follow the same pattern of growth, the telecommunications infrastructure (at present about nine years behind the EC average) may remain a brake on IS developments.

The state-owned academic Internet provider Arnes has expanded to become a business-oriented service provider, connecting universities, schools, research institutions and libraries. Since 1996 several other Internet providers have emerged, including services by Telekom Slovenije.

Conclusion

In view of the highly advanced infrastructure combined with the excellence of the national education system, we can expect Slovenia to realise potentialities of the Information Society earlier than the average CEEC.

Education, Training and Youth

Articles 126 and 127 of the EC Treaty provide that the Community shall contribute to the development of quality education and implement a vocational training policy aimed at promoting the European dimension in education and at enhancing industrial adaptation and the responsiveness of the labour market through vocational training policies.

The Europe Agreement provides for cooperation in raising the level of education and professional qualifications.

The White Paper includes no measures in this field.

Descriptive Summary

Slovenia's spending on education amounts to 5,8 % of GDP. It takes 12,6 % of the state budget.

There are 820 schools, 305 000 pupils, 40 000 students and 23 000 teachers in Slovenia.

Since 1990 policy priorities have been gradually refocused to cope with the needs of a free market economy aiming mainly at strengthening links between education and training on the one hand, and the labour market on the other.

The 1996 White Paper on Education in the Republic of Slovenia sets the framework for comprehensive legal reform of the national education and training system. On this basis, six acts have been adopted which regulate (1) the organisation and funding of education, (2) pre-school education, (3) primary schools, (4) gymnasia, (5) vocational education and training and (6) adult education. A Higher Education Act was adopted in 1993 which focused on the restructuring of universities and the development of non-university institutions for higher professional and vocational education.

The Tempus programme has contributed to the achievement of the goals of higher education reform and created the basis for cooperation with the EU higher education institutions.

About 15 % of the total population of Slovenia is between 15 and 25 (age group eligible for the Youth for Europe programme). Several measures in the field of youth have been taken in the past years to strengthen the role of youth associations in society and to provide premises for youth activities. A national youth information and counselling centre, and its network at local level, have been established and youth mobility and volunteer services are supported. Slovenia should start participating in the Youth for Europe programme in 1998.

Current and Prospective Assessment

The Slovene Government made significant progress in re-orienting the education and training system towards a human resources development policy which is suitable for a small open market economy aiming at international competitiveness. Further efforts remain to be undertaken in the field of policy implementation.

As regards education, budgetary resources should now be re-oriented in line with the new priorities identified. In addition, there is scope for intensifying links with research and development and strengthening orientations towards market developments.

Slovenia should start participation in the Youth for Europe programme in 1998, subject to the ratification of the Europe Agreement. The Youth for Europe National Agency has not yet been designated.

Conclusion

In the perspective of accession, no major problems should be expected in these fields.

Research and Technological Development

Research and Technological Development activities at Community level, as provided for by the Treaty and in the Framework Programme, aim at improving the competitiveness of European industry, the quality of life, as well as supporting sustainable development, environmental protection, and other common policies.

The Europe Agreement will provide for cooperation in these areas, notably through participation in the Framework Programme.

The White Paper includes no direct measures in this field.

Descriptive Summary

The national policy for research and technological development is defined in the National Research programme adopted in January 1995. Basic legislation in this sector is the Law on Research Activities established in 1991 which is to be replaced by a new Law on Financing and Organisations in the Field of Science and technology currently under preparation by the Ministry of Science and Technology.

The current science expenditure amounted to 1,77 % of GDP in 1995 (up from 1,46 % in 1993), of which 0,75 % by private enterprises. The Slovenian Government's aim to increase this rate to 2,5 % by 2000 will require substantial investments by both the public and the private sector.

Two universities and more than 40 research institutes compete for limited funds. At the same time, there is an overall tendency to decrease public financial support. In addition, there are about 20 private foundations providing general support and fellowships for the development of the sector. The Academy of Science and Art and the National Council for Research and Development have advisory functions on policy.

A programme with priority setting in science and technology policy and encouragement measures to link with industry has been set up. Core priorities are improved targeting of financial support, increased private funding, enhanced participation in international research programmes, refocusing of budgetary allocations towards enterprise targeted applied research and improved know how-transfer.

Regular cooperation with the European Community started in 1992 with the Third Research and Technology Development Framework Programme. So far, cooperation was mainly concentrated on Copernicus (Specific Programme for Cooperation with CECs and NIS) and remains rather low for participation in the Fourth Framework Programme. Slovenia is a member of Cost (European cooperation in the field of scientific and technical research) and Eureka (European Research Coordination Agency).

Since 1993, the statistics in this field are compatible with OECD standards.

Current and Prospective Assessment

The overall re-organisation of the complex research and technological development structures has advanced and aims at intensifying links with economic and industrial development. However, considerable efforts remain to be undertaken to revitalize technological development in the industrial sector and to exploit the potential of national research for economic development. Privatisation of research institutes is supported. Additional financial resources are provided for research and networking infrastructure, guarantees and capital investments as seed or venture capital. So far, this had not led to the results expected, but there are reasonable prospects for an upturn.

Slovenia has declared its interest in full association with the Fifth Framework Programme.

Conclusion

In the perspective of accession, no major problems are expected in this field. Accession would be of mutual benefit.

Telecommunications

The objectives of EC telecommunications policy are the elimination of obstacles to the effective operation of the Single Market in telecommunications equipment, services and networks, the opening of foreign markets to EU companies and the achievement of universally available modern services for EU residents and businesses. These are achieved through harmonisation of the standards and conditions for service offerings the liberalisation of the markets for terminals, services and networks and the adoption of necessary regulatory instruments. The Directives and policies needed to achieve this have now been established, but the liberalisation of public voice telephony and operation of related infrastructure will be deferred for a year or two after 1998 in certain Member States.

The Europe Agreement provides for cooperation aimed at enhancing standards and practices towards EC levels in telecommunication and postal policies, standardisation, regulatory approaches and the modernisation of infrastructure.

The White Paper focuses on the approximation of regulation, networks and services, followed by further steps ensuring gradual sector liberalisation.

Descriptive Summary

Slovenia emerged from independence with its telecommunications system intact. The telephone line penetration rate increased from 24,1 % in 1991 to 33,3 % at present. The digitalisation rate of the network is well advanced and reached 66 % of the transmission and 46 % of the switching capacity by mid 1995.

The current legislation and regulatory instruments are the previous Yugoslav law on Telecommunications Systems of 1988; a new law on telecommunications of May 1997 and the decree of 1995 on Type Approval, Certification and Testing of Terminal Equipment. The public operator Telekom Slovenije has a monopoly of voice telephony until the year 2000. It also has a subsidiary which runs the two mobile telephony networks with analogue and digital standards. Other services are liberalised. The state ownership of Telekom Slovenije amounts to 76 % and will be further reduced by about one third to make the organisation more flexible and commercial.

Current and Prospective Assessment

Degree of Liberalisation

While there has been little progression in liberalisation, recent Government declarations indicate that market opening is accelerating which will create a major challenge for Telekom Slovenije. The public operator has exclusive rights for the fixed network and voice telephony until 1 January 2001. A subsidiary of the operator is running the two mobile telephony networks with analogue and digital standards. The markets for value added services are liberalised. The Government intends to publish a tender for a second GSM mobile telephony network at the end of 1997.

Approximation to EC law

A new telecommunications law was adopted by Parliament on 28 May 1997. The conformity of the final legislation as voted by Parliament with EU-law is being checked. A Decree on Type Approval, Certification and Testing of Terminal Equipment was issued in 1995. After the adoption of the Decrees for the application of the

Telecommunications Law and the adoption of the draft frequency allocation Decree, it can be expected that the country will harmonise the remaining part of its regulation with the *acquis* by 2000. The administrative capacity to handle these approximation requirements needs further strengthening.

In June 1997 the Government started to adjust the distorted tariffs structure by increasing the tariffs for local communications (plus 9 %) and by reducing the tariffs for other phone calls (minus 18 %). The local call price is among the lowest of the region but there is a very high connection charge for new customers. Universal service remains to be achieved and, as competition develops and the network expands into less advanced areas, the existence of obligations on operators to provide universal service will undoubtedly become a focus of regulatory activity.

Infrastructure

The penetration rate in the telephone service increased from 24,1 in 1991 to 33,3 per 100 inhabitants in 1997 (the average in Ireland, Portugal and Greece is about 43,9 per 100) and the digitisation rate in 1997 is 66 % (the average in Ireland, Portugal and Greece is about 62,4). ISDN services have been introduced in two major cities since 1995. By the end of the year 2000, the penetration rate for telephony is planned to reach 40 %. The full digitisation of the transit network is not expected to be completed until the year 2010. There are about 220 000 CATV subscribers corresponding to 90 % of the households connected (100 network operators).

There is little direct foreign investment so far in the telecommunications sector. The only operator of mobile telephony, Mobitel, is a 100 % subsidiary of Telekom Slovenije and the paging operator, Teleray, is a private Slovenian company. In 1996 Telekom Slovenije received an 35 million ECU loan from a consortium of foreign banks.

Competitiveness of the Sector

In 1995 there were 5 employees per 1 000 lines (the average in Ireland, Portugal and Greece is about 6,2) and the average waiting time for a telephone line was 1,8 years. The price of a standard telephone line for business communications (283 ECU) is at a medium level compared to the prices in the region. The revenue per line (about 344 ECU in 1995) is the highest in the region. This should be sufficient to ensure that Telekom Slovenije can be run as a business profitable enough to allow for further investment. However, the sector will only be able to face full competition if substantial efforts are made towards more cost-oriented tariffs.

Conclusion

Telecommunications in Slovenia, with a modern infrastructure and advanced service, in the mid term will reach a level comparable to some of the EU Member States. Implementing the *acquis* will be possible in the medium term but will require early introduction of competition in all fields. The public network operator should be able to face full competition if tariff rebalancing is implemented before 2000.

Audio-visual

The audio-visual *acquis* aims, in the context of the internal market, for the provision and free movement of audio-visual services within the EU as well as the promotion of the European programme industry. The Television Without Frontiers Directive, which is applicable to all broadcasters regardless of the modes of transmission (terrestrial, satellite, cable) or their private or public nature, contains this *acquis*, setting down basic rules concerning transfrontier broadcasting. The main points are: to ensure the free movement of television broadcasts throughout Member States; to promote the production and distribution of European audio-visual works (by laying down a minimum proportion of broadcasting time for European works and those by independent producers); to set basic standards in the field of television advertising; to provide for the protection of minors and to allow for the right of reply.

The Europe Agreement provides for cooperation in the promotion and modernisation of the audio-visual industry, and the harmonisation of regulatory aspects of audio-visual policy.

The Television Without Frontiers Directives is a Stage I measure in the White Paper.

Descriptive Summary

The legal framework for the audio-visual sector is determined by the Law on Public Media, and the 1994 Law on Radio and Television Slovenia.

The main television broadcaster is the public service RTV Slovenia, although a number of other television organisations also operate in the market.

Financial assistance is provided to productions made under a special system of cofinancing. Budgetary finance is provided to encourage investment in independent productions, European works and national productions in the area of film and video. Detailed information on film distribution is not available.

Current and Prospective Assessment

The audio-visual sector in Slovenia is attempting to re-establish itself after major upheavals in recent years, and is characterised by rapid growth and constant change. Its ability properly to adhere to the *acquis* presupposes an upgrading of the capacity of the programme-making industry to meet the important challenges of an adapted regulatory framework.

Slovenian audio-visual legislation is partially compatible with EU requirements; deficiencies remain in a number of areas, including freedom of reception, the promotion of European works, independent producers and recent works, isolated advertising spots, the protection of minors, and advertising rules. The Slovenian Government has stated its intention that laws bringing Slovenia into line with EU requirements should be passed in 1998.

Conclusion

Provided that the necessary legislative measures are pursued in the timescale foreseen and are accompanied by necessary structural adaptation of the industry, Slovenia should be able to meet EC requirements in the audio-visual sector in the medium term.

3.3. Economic and Fiscal Affairs

Economic and Monetary Union

By the time of Slovenia's accession, the third stage of EMU will have commenced. This will mark important changes for all Member States, including those that do not participate in the euro area. All Member States, including the new ones, will participate fully in the Economic and Monetary Union. Their economic policies will be a matter of common concern and they will be involved in the coordination of economic policies (national convergence programmes, broad economic guidelines, multilateral surveillance, excessive deficit procedure). They will be required to respect the stability and growth pact, to renounce any direct central bank financing of the public sector deficit and privileged access of public authorities to financial institutions, and to have completed the liberalisation of capital movements.

Accession means closer monetary and exchange rate cooperation with the European Union. This will require strengthening structural reforms in the area of monetary and exchange rate policies. Member States not participating in the euro area will be able to conduct an autonomous monetary policy and participate in the European System of Central Banks (ESCB) on a restricted basis. Their central banks have to be independent and have price stability as their primary objective. Monetary policy has to be conducted with market-based instruments and has to be 'efficient' in transmitting its impulses to the real economy. Therefore, reforms need to be pursued to tackle factors that hinder the efficiency of monetary policy, such as the lack of competition in the banking sector, the lack of development of financial markets and the problem of 'bad loans' in the banking sector. Finally all Member States shall treat their exchange rate policy as a matter of common interest and be in a position to stabilise their exchange rates in a mechanism yet to be decided.

As membership of the European Union implies acceptance of the goal of EMU, the convergence criteria will have to be fulfilled by Slovenia, although not necessarily on accession. While the fulfilment of the convergence criteria is not a precondition for EU membership, they remain key points of reference for stability oriented macroeconomic policies, and must in time be fulfilled by new Member States on a permanent basis. Hence the successful conclusion of systematic transformation and market oriented structural reforms is essential. Slovenia's economic situation and progress has already been analysed in preceding chapters of this Opinion.

Current and Prospective Assessment

The Slovenian Central Bank enjoys a relatively high degree of independence from the Government. The Governor is appointed by the Parliament and the Bank is the only institution responsible for monetary policy actions. The formal objective of the Central Bank is the stability of the domestic currency and implicitly price stability. The Law on the Central Bank is not fully compatible with the Treaty prohibition of budget deficit financing, but the sound fiscal record to date has eliminated the need for central bank deficit financing.

Monetary policy in Slovenia has been quite effective in reducing inflation. The 1996 inflation rate was at the single digit level. However, the efficiency of monetary policy is hindered by several different factors. The privatisation of state-owned banks and the restructuring of the whole banking sector has proceeded well after a relatively slow start. The bad loans, although reduced, remain a problem. The lack of government bonds papers, due to the sound fiscal record, makes it difficult for the Central Bank to use indirect instruments for the purpose of money supply control. In addition, the policy of preserving the high degree of indexation of the economy keeps lending interest rates high, thus discouraging financial intermediation and the ability of monetary policy to affect the real economy. The high degree of indexation is also responsible for the occurrence of massive speculative capital inflows. These capital inflows endanger the ability of the Central Bank to control monetary aggregates. They also slow down the disinflationary process. Moreover, if they are sterilised they are the source of additional budgetary expenditures. Finally, they are always subject to possible reversal and put the country's currency under severe strains. In early 1996, the Slovenian authorities have introduced capital

controls to limit this phenomenon. These measures which are in contradiction to the Europe agreement are still operational.

The Slovenian exchange rate regime has been a managed float since mid-1992. In practice the Slovenian tolar has shadowed the Deutsche Mark. The exchange rate policy combined with a positive inflation differential and a highly indexed economy, led to a massive speculative capital inflow in the period 1992-1994. In 1995, the Slovenian authorities relaxed their exchange rate stance and after an initial appreciation, the exchange rate has been depreciating slowly. The current account is virtually balanced.

Conclusion

It is premature to judge whether Slovenia will be in a position, by the time of its accession, to participate in the euro area; that will depend on the success of its structural transformation permitting to attain and to adhere permanently to the convergence criteria, which are not however a condition of accession.

Slovenia's participation in the third stage of EMU as a non-participant in the euro area should pose no problems in the medium term. However, it is important that central bank legislation is made fully compatible with EC rules and that the banking sector is restructured. Finally, monetary policies able to curb speculative capital inflows without resorting systematically to capital controls should be adopted.

Taxation

The *acquis* in the area of direct taxation mainly concerns some aspects of corporation taxes and capital duty. The four freedoms of the EC Treaty have a wider impact on national tax systems.

The indirect taxation *acquis* consists primarily of harmonised legislation in the field of Value Added Tax and excise duties. This includes the application of a non-cumulative general tax on consumption (VAT) which is levied on all stages of production and distribution of goods and services. This implies an equal tax treatment of domestic and non-domestic (import) transactions. The VAT *acquis* also contains transitional arrangements for the taxation of transactions within the European Union between taxable persons. In the field of excise duties the *acquis* contains harmonised tax structures and minimum rates of duty together with common rules on the holding and movement of harmonised excisable goods (including the use of fiscal warehouses). As a result of the introduction of the Single Market, all fiscal controls at the Community's internal frontiers were abolished in January 1993.

The mutual assistance between Member State tax authorities is an important feature of administrative co-operation in the internal market; the respective Directive covers both direct and indirect taxation.

The Europe Agreement contains provisions on approximation of legislation in the area of indirect taxation.

The White Paper contains as Stage I measures those which make up the main requirements of the indirect taxation *acquis* (essentially, those measures applied in the Community up to 1993), and as Stage II measures those which are in addition necessary to implement the full indirect taxation *acquis*.

Descriptive Summary

Direct Taxation

The two company taxation Directives and the Arbitration Convention provide for a mechanism which applies on the basis of reciprocity. Respective provisions can therefore by definition not be expected to exist before accession.

Indirect Taxation

Nearly 70 % of the fiscal revenue over the past four years has been generated through indirect taxes (i.e. the sales tax and customs duties) and this has continued on an upward trend.

Value Added Tax

At present Slovenia does not operate a Value Added Tax system. Instead it operates a system of single-stage sales tax on final consumption which bears little resemblance to the value added system applied within the Community.

Excise

Slovenia does not yet have a system of excise duty. Instead, *ad valorem* rates of duty apply on mineral oils, alcoholic beverages and tobacco products except cigarettes.

Mutual Assistance

The tax administration has not yet had to develop its capacity for mutual assistance with the tax authorities of Member States, since mutual assistance is a feature which would only become applicable on accession.

Current and Prospective Assessment

Value Added Tax

Slovenia's membership of the European Union would require the introduction of a Community based VAT system. The current Slovenian draft VAT law has been based upon the main principles of the Community VAT system but will require some additional adjustments to bring the VAT legislation into line with the requirements of the Community *acquis*.

The Slovenian national strategy plan for implementing the recommendations of the White Paper regarding VAT envisages the introduction of a VAT system. A proposal for the introduction of a VAT system has been submitted to the Slovenian National Assembly for adoption. The VAT Act is planned to enter into force on 1 January 1999.

Excise

The current excise duty system does not comply with Community requirements, and it discriminates against certain imported commodities in favour of domestically produced products.

A draft law on excise duty has been prepared and is going through the Slovenian National Assembly with an anticipated implementation date of 1 January 1999. The section dealing with scope, coverage and exemptions is comprehensive and in accord with the terms of the EC Directives relating to harmonisation of the structures of excise duties. The section dealing with procedures is less well developed. It provides for the introduction of intra-warehouse movement under suspension of duty, and an accompanying document system on the lines of the document required by the Community excise legislation.

It will be important to ensure that the excise tax reform will be fully implemented and effectively operated in a way which is consistent with the EC provisions on the holding and movement of goods.

Mutual Assistance

There would also be a need, on accession, to implement the appropriate arrangements for administrative cooperation and mutual assistance between Member States. These requirements are essential for the functioning of the internal market.

Conclusion

The *acquis* in respect of direct taxation should present no significant difficulties.

Although legislation is in preparation, in the absence at present of a VAT or excise system it must remain open to doubt whether Slovenia could comply with the *acquis* in the medium term.

It should be possible to start participating in mutual assistance as the tax administration develops its expertise in this respect.

Statistics

The main principles of the Community *acquis* relate to the impartiality, reliability, transparency, confidentiality (of individual information) and dissemination of official statistics. In addition there exists an important body of principles and practices concerning the use of European and international classifications, systems of national accounts, business registers, and various categories of statistics.

The Europe Agreement provides for cooperation to develop effective and reliable statistics, in harmony with international standards and classifications.

The White Paper includes no provisions in this field.

Descriptive Summary

The Statistical Office of Slovenia (SO) is the central body charged with producing and disseminating official statistics in Slovenia.

The legal basis for Slovene official statistics consists of the 1995 Law on National Statistics.

Current and Prospective Assessment

Slovene legislation is, with very few exceptions, compatible with the current standards applied within the European Union.

Some issues of confidentiality need clarification, and there are deficiencies in sectors such as financial accounts, agricultural statistics, and foreign trade statistics.

Conclusion

Slovenia should be able to comply with EU requirements for official statistics within the next few years.

3.4. Sectoral Policies

Industry

EC industrial policy seeks to enhance competitiveness, thus achieving rising living standards and high rates of employment. It aims at speeding up adjustment to structural change, encouraging an environment favourable to initiative, to the development of undertakings throughout the Community, and to industrial cooperation, and fostering better exploitation of the industrial potential of policies of innovation, research and technological development. EU industrial policy is horizontal by nature. Sectoral communications aim at transposing horizontal concepts into specific sectors. EC industrial policy results from an articulation of instruments from a number of Community policies; it includes both instruments related to the operation of markets (product specification and market access, trade policy, state aids and competitions policy) and measures related to industry's capacity to adapt to change (stable macroeconomic environment, technology, training, etc.).

In order to cope with competitive pressure and market forces within the Union, the industry of applicant countries needs to have achieved a certain level of competitiveness by the time of accession. The applicant countries need to be seen as pursuing policies aimed at open and competitive markets along the lines set out in Article 130 ('Industry') of the Treaty. Cooperation between the EC and the candidate countries in the fields of industrial cooperation, investment, industrial standardisation and conformity assessment as provided for in the Europe Agreement is an important indicator of development in the right direction.

Descriptive Summary

Slovenia has a small industrial sector, commensurate with the size of the country. The total production of Slovene industry is at present in the order of 5,3 billion ECU or less than twice the industrial production of Luxembourg, and its share in GDP has decreased from 37 % in 1990 to 32 % in 1995. The manufacturing sector consists of slightly more than 8 000 enterprises of which more than 90 % are private owned; several hundreds of enterprises are still 'socially-owned'. As yet there is no statutory legislation established for state-owned enterprises which cover about 30 % of the Slovene economy. The degree of concentration is high as 570 companies account for 80 % of industrial employment, turnout and exports. The most important sectors

are chemicals, electrical and mechanical engineering, automotive products, textiles and clothing, and paper and wood products.

Slovenia has managed to build on its past position as the most sophisticated manufacturing centre of former Yugoslavia where its industries specialised in, processing raw materials and semi-manufactured goods from the southern republics. Its post-independence recovery has so far largely been a success story recovering well from the loss of most of its former Yugoslav markets. The industry has become more export oriented and the import regime is liberal. The Government is committed to further liberalisation and elimination of non-tariff barriers. Horizontal support policies, in particular as regards small and medium enterprises, regional development and enterprise targeted research and development, are still at an early stage of development.

However, industrial production slowed down in 1995 and 1996, due *inter alia* to weak demand in some key export markets, the high level of the tolar and reduced competitiveness in terms of labour costs. Other factors which have contributed are high interest rates, foreign capital restrictions, and slow legislative adaptation. As a result, investment levels and modernisation of industry have suffered. Sectors particularly affected are paper, textiles and clothing, leather, food products, iron and steel, printing; however, other sectors such as electrical engineering, non-ferrous metal processing, chemicals and wood products operate relatively well.

Privatisation of Slovene industry has run into some difficulty, although many companies are

Slovene industry, main production sectors in 1995

Sector	% Share industrial GVA	Number of companies	% Share industrial Employment
Raw material processing (steel, metallurgy, cement, glass, ceramic, paper, wood)	18	924	17,5
Mechanical and electronic engineering	15,5	1 027	20
Textiles, clothing, leather/shoes	9	624	14
Foodstuffs	7	280	6
Automotive	5	1	5
Chemicals	6	468	5
Pharmaceuticals	5,5	12	2
Information technologies	2,5	332	2,5
Total	100		100
Industrial production as % of GDP	*32*		

well managed and relatively well equipped, mainly due to the complexity of the mix of a voucher system, management buy-out options, and other methods. Public utilities have not been privatised so far. Foreign direct investment is relatively low (1 % of GDP), despite very little perceived political risk.

In comparison with other CEECs the productivity of *basic sectors* (metallurgy, steel, glass, ceramics, wood-paper cement) is relatively high. The industrial structure in these sectors is characterised by a predominance of SMEs. There are no important capacity surpluses. Privatisation is advanced in most of these sectors.

The *steel industry* is very small and privatisation is slow. Slovenia shows a relatively high degree of specialisation and strong export capacity in the *non-ferrous metals sectors* (in particular aluminium), but also in *tires* and *paper*.

Slovenia has an advantage in having a more modern *forest-based industries sector* than neighbouring CEECs and a correspondingly higher level of inward investment, especially from EU companies. The sector is small but quality is often on EU level (in particular for pulps, paper and printing applications). Hence, Slovenia can be considered as an emerging competitor to EU producers in some niche markets in the paper sector, as witnessed by significant exports. The high level of privatisation has been an important factor behind this positive performance.

Textile and clothing: the majority of the companies in this industry are SMEs but production is concentrated in a few major companies. Net investments in clothing correspond to disinvestment in the textile subsector, indicating a specialisation down-stream of the production chain. Wage costs are among the highest in the CEECs (although still lower than in the EU). FDI is focusing on new technologies and equipment modernisation. The textile and clothing industry is already integrated into the European 'filière' especially because of widespread outward processing trade (OPT), which underlies three quarters of total exports of clothing.

Foodstuffs industry: this sector is small in relation to the size of the market, highly fragmented, and weak.

The only *automotive* producer of importance is a subsidiary of a French car producer.

Chemicals: this sector is small and Slovenia does not have any major petrochemical activities. However, there is a major tire production facility established as a joint venture with a German/Austrian producer which is the state of the art and a major exporter.

The *pharmaceutical industry* is one of the largest in Central Europe. Production is highly concentrated in three companies. About 75 % of production is exported, mainly to the CEECs. Slovenian firms have also begun to market some generic drugs in EU markets. The sector fully harmonised with relevant EC legislation and product patent protection has been introduced. Enforcement remains a problem, however.

The *information technology (IT)* industry is small but in good shape. It has emerged from ex-Yugoslavia's long-term technological development programme which placed electronics as a priority of national economic development. Slovenia has a remarkable tradition in electrical and electronic consumer products (both brown and white products), with substantial exports to the EU. Production is mainly based on licences from major multinationals

Demand forecasts for the IT sector in Slovenia are optimistic. The leading company for production of telecom equipment can probably participate further in the world-wide growth as it supplies major global corporations with components and assemblies.

Current and Prospective Assessment

Slovenian industry started from a productivity level that was much higher than in the other applicant countries and which is probably already now comparable to that of some Member States. However, progress has been slow over the last few years, due to an only moderate investment rate and slow privatisation. FDI has been limited by restriction on land ownership, capital controls and slow privatisation and has so far financed only about 5 % of all investment, one of the lowest rate in all applicant countries.

While transformation of ownership has advanced in the majority of socially-owned companies, their restructuring is in most cases still to be undertaken. Obstacles are the undercapitalisation of enterprises due to the prevailing pattern of management buy-outs and the high real interest rates which are aimed at avoiding large current account deficits and keeping inflation under control, but which curb enterprise investment. The national authorities will also need to define a proper strategy for the future management or privatisation of state-owned enterprises and public utilities. Effective regulatory systems are to be set up. There is scope for improving the quality and efficiency of the services to the public and private sector. Continued price liberalisation would further support the efficient allocation of resources. Foreign investments could play an important role to improve competition and efficiency.

In early 1997 the Slovenian Government presented its new strategy for increasing the competitiveness of Slovenian industry which sets out a wide range of measures compatible with the orientations given by Article 130 of the Treaty. Implementation has started recently, though partly by way of measures incompatible with EC disciplines such as on state aid control. Further progress on industrial competitiveness depends on implementation of the strategy, by both industry itself and the Slovene Government.

Conclusion on Industrial Competitiveness

The current level and perspective for competitiveness of most of the Slovene industry enables a positive expectation on its capacity to cope with the competitive pressure and market forces within the Union in the medium term. There may however be problems linked to certain labour market rigidities and for those sectors and companies which have not yet undergone restructuring.

An evaluation of the *acquis* specific to the free circulation of industrial goods is to be found in the separate section on the internal market.

Agriculture

The Common Agricultural Policy aims to maintain and develop a modern agricultural system ensuring a fair standard of living for the agricultural community and the supply of goods at a reasonable price for consumers, and ensuring the free movement of goods within the EC. Special attention is given to the environment and rural development. Common Market Organisations exist to administer the CAP. These are comple-

mented by regulations on veterinary health, plant health and animal nutrition and by regulations concerning food hygiene. Legislation also exists in the area of structural policy, originally developed primarily to modernise and enlarge agriculture, but more recently with an increasing emphasis on the environment, and the regional differentiation of the policy. Since reforms in 1992, increasing contributions to farm support have come from direct aid payments compensating cuts in support prices.

The Europe Agreement provides the basis for agricultural trade between Slovenia and the Community and aims to promote cooperation on the modernisation, restructuring of Slovenia's agriculture sector as well as the agro-industrial sector and plant health standards. Prior to ratification of this Agreement, the Interim Agreement is regulating a preferential trade in the field of agriculture.

The White Paper covers the fields of veterinary, plant health and animal nutrition controls, as well as marketing requirements for individual commodities. The purpose of such legislation is to protect consumers, public health and the health of animals and plants.

Descriptive Summary

Agricultural Situation

The value of the agricultural production 1995 was approximately 0,56 % of that of the Union.

Agriculture has a modest place in Slovenia in terms of GDP, employment and export earnings. However, it plays an important role as an economic and social stabiliser. Agriculture accounts for 4,3 % of the GDP and around 7 % of employment.

About 92 % of the agricultural land is privately owned while the remaining 8 % is owned by the State. There are 156 000 holdings in Slovenia, of which 8 % have less than 10 hectares. About 46 000 of these holdings are household plots. The Slovenian farm sector therefore faces a substantial challenge of structural adjustment, particularly in sectors without price support measures in the EC (pig, poultry and egg production).

Out of a total area of 2 million hectares about 50 % is covered by forest and about 39 % is agricultural land. About 70 % of the agricultural land is in less-favoured hilly and mountainous regions, mainly used for permanent pasture. Only 30 % of the agricultural area, or 250 000 hectares, is arable land.

The most important arable crops are cereals (45 % of arable land), fodder (30 %) and potatoes (10 %). Agricultural production is equally shared between crop (52 %) and livestock production (48 %).

Slovenia is a net importer of food and agricultural products (self-sufficiency: 84 %). In 1995 it produced 535 000 tonnes cereals, 449 000 tonnes potatoes, 65 000 tonnes sugar (included imported raw sugar for processing), 700 000 hectoliters wine, 590 000 tonnes milk, 36 000 tonnes beef, 58 000 tonnes pigmeat and 56 000 tonnes poultry meat. The most important sectors producing surplus for exports are wine, hops, poultry and dairy. However the external trade in agricultural products represents a limited role in the overall trade balance (4 % of exports, 8,2 % of imports). The total agricultural imports amount to 612 million ECU and the export to 262 million ECU. While the EC is an increasingly important trading partner in agricultural products (EU-15: 55 % of imports, 30 % of exports) the former Yugoslavia remains Slovenias most important export market (53 % of export in 1996).

Although the agro-food industry is relatively well structured and benefits for the most part from the same technological methods as used in the EC, the industry is suffering from low utilisation of capacity and would need to adapt to EU-quality standards.

However the privatisation process has not been completed. About 10 % of the sector has not yet been privatised, amongst which the most important companies.

Agricultural Policy

Slovenia started to implement its own agricultural policy in 1991. This policy was consolidated with the adoption of the 'Strategy for Agricultural Development of Slovenia' in 1993 putting special emphasis on sustainable rural and agricultural development with recognition of ecological and social aspects. The support policies include the following main elements a) price control for milk, sugar, wheat and flour; b) input

subsidies, credit and investment support; c) external border protection an export aid.

Agricultural prices in Slovenia are generally higher than in other CECs, and in most cases higher than the lowest price registered in the EU markets. Wheat prices are substantially higher than EC prices due to higher support prices for bread making wheat in Slovenia.

The main policy measures in sectors with market organisations are similar, or close to, EC policies. However, a number of sectors have very few market intervention mechanisms other than external trade protection. Rural development is an essential element of Slovenian agricultural policy, and a number of the policy measures are aimed at attenuating unfavourable production conditions for farmers in hilly and mountainous regions and promoting extra-agricultural economic activity such as production of higher value-added speciality products, tourism, etc.

Slovenia is in the process of reviewing its agricultural policy with the objective of bringing it closer to the CAP. Direct payments, such as income aid for farmers, together with regional and rural development policies, are envisaged to be gradually introduced. Changes in the price support measures for milk were adopted in 1996. With envisaged implementation in 1997, direct payments replace price policy supporting milk production in mountainous and hilly areas.

The share of the government's budget spent on agriculture is about 2 %. Increased spending is envisaged by the new government in conjunction with the planned implementation of policy measures similar to the CAP (direct payment, rural development policies).

Foreign trade policy represents an important element in Slovenian food and agricultural policy. In 1993 Slovenia introduced a system of threshold prices and variable import levies. When Slovenia became a member of the WTO these measures were changed in accordance with the conditions of the GATT Agreement. Slovenia has undertaken the commitments of the GATT Agreement on domestic support, market access and export subsidies. Slovenia has made its commitments in ECUs. The limited export subsidies used so far are envisaged to be used for export promotion activities. The Europe Agreement with Slovenia was signed in 1996.

Slovenia is also a member of CEFTA (Central Europe Free Trade Agreement). Agricultural market liberalisation within CEFTA will be implemented progressively with the intention of achieving in 1999 complete market integration between the contracting parties.

Slovenian trade policy is also aimed at maintaining and restoring its markets in the former Yugoslavian Republics. In this framework, a free trade agreement has been signed with the Former Yugoslavian Republic of Macedonia (FYROM).

Slovenia is introducing the legislation identified in the White Paper.

Current and Prospective Assessment

A major concern of the Slovenian Government is the pressure for structural adjustment in the farming sector, in particular in the mountainous regions and less favoured areas. To the extent to which Slovenia achieves its objectives of bringing its policies closer to the CAP in major sectors, there should not be major difficulties for Slovenia adapting to EC policies. However, domestic budget and human resources constraints could delay the process of approximation.

Adjustments of certain market organisations are necessary. a) State monopolies in the cereals, oilseed and sugar sector will have to be dismantled; b) the Slovenian sugar policy would need to be adapted to EC policies; c) the policies in the pigmeat, poultry and egg sectors are similar to EC policies and these sectors do not represent any major obstacle for accession if a new draft legislation introducing intervention prices and public intervention purchases in the pigmeat sector is not approved by Parliament; d) the policies applied to the dairy and beef sectors are different from EC policies on essential points (dairy quotas, market price quotation systems, etc.).

The main market policy instruments applied in the EC are not applied in Slovenia. This includes key instruments such as dairy quotas, key features of the arable crop scheme (base area, set-aside, compensatory payments and premiums in the livestock sector), as well as certain rural and structural development programmes. Management and control of these measures would require relatively sophisticated administrative systems, including an appropriate land register and cattle identification and registration systems.

It is difficult to foresee at this stage what will be the development of agricultural support prices in Slovenia in the period before accession; this will depend on a number of factors including the domestic economy, the situation on export markets, and the development of price support levels in the Union. However the Slovenian Government has announced its intention to decrease support prices and move towards more targeted direct income support.

An important element in Slovenian agricultural policy is support to reducing costs of production and income support in disadvantageous areas. Some of these policies, in particular direct input subsidies, are in conflict with the *acquis* while other policies (credit and investment policies) are within the scope of EC policies for structural development.

The food processing sector could be the most affected by membership. It is essential that appropriate policies on increasing quality standards and productivity will be pursued during the pre-accession period. The increased trade liberalisation resulting from regional trade agreements will likely accelerate the adjustment process through increased competition.

Slovenia has made progress in implementing the key measures identified in the White Paper. With a continuation of current progress the most essential parts of internal market measures should be in place by the end of the decade. However, it is difficult at this stage to assess the degree of approximation to the *acquis* and to what extent the necessary inspection and control infrastructure is, or will be, in place to ensure adequate enforcement of the legislation.

In the veterinary field approximation to, and an implementation of the *acquis* has been partly achieved. The indicated timetables for the approval and implementation of secondary legislation in the different sections vary from 1997 until the year 2000. It is questionable whether the legal structure is sufficiently adequate to amend/implement EC legislation effectively.

In the approximation process, further adoption would be needed with regard to the concept of HACCP (Hazard Analysis Critical Control Point) and auto-control, monitoring and surveillance programs, disease eradication, internal market control measures (safeguard, the license system, veterinary checks, additional guarantees, regionalisation), import regime (approved third countries, approved establishments) and the identification and registration system of animals (particularly back yard holdings). The facilities and professional experience at border inspection posts and veterinary laboratories need upgrading. The computerised information system, the identification and registration system of animals, and the rendering infrastructure need to be improved. Vaccination against classical swine fever is still being carried out and a change to a non vaccination policy is necessary but will be technically difficult.

As regards seeds and propagation material, plant health, plant protection products, pesticide residues and animal nutrition, the approximation of legislation is underway. However it will be necessary for the Commission to verify whether the legislation is correctly implemented.

EC marketing standards for fruit and vegetables would need to be introduced. Legislation is currently being prepared to harmonize marketing requirements in the wine sector. Slovenia is a member of the OIV (Office international de la vigne et du vin) and its legislation is harmonised with OIV resolutions.

The administration has limited management experience, and at the present stage the administrative structure appears to be inadequate to ensure appropriate implementation and enforcement of the *acquis*.

Conclusion

Further alignment to the *acquis* is still necessary although significant progress has been made in adopting the measures mentioned in the White Paper.

Particular efforts are needed in relation to:

☐ strengthening of structural and rural development policy;

☐ implementation and enforcement of veterinary and plant health requirements and upgrading of establishments to meet EC standards; this is particularly important with regard to the inspection and control arrangements for protecting the EU external border;

☐ strengthening of the administrative structures to ensure the necessary capacity to implement and enforce the policy instruments of the CAP;

☐ further restructuring of the agro-food sector to improve its competitive capacity.

If such progress is accomplished, accession in the medium term should not be accompanied by significant problems in applying the common agricultural policy in an appropriate manner.

Fisheries

The Common Fisheries Policy includes common market organisations, structural policy, agreements with third countries, management and conservation of fish resources, and scientific research in support of these activities.

The Europe Agreement includes provisions concerning trade in fisheries products with the Community.

The White Paper includes no measures in this field.

Descriptive Summary

The fishing sector does not play an important role in the national economy. Along the Adriatic coast it has local significance but the limited fishing opportunities offered by the Adriatic mean that it will remain small-scale. In 1995, 105 vessels caught 1 911 tonnes (mostly pilchard, anchovy, sprat). Only 183 fishermen were employed.

As a trading partner of the Community, Slovenia represents 0,05 % of EU total imports (independently of origin) of fisheries products and 2 % of EU imports of fisheries products from the candidate countries alone (in terms of value). As regards EU exports, Slovenia receives 0,52 % of our total exports of fisheries products and 6,2 % of our exports of these products to the candidate countries (in terms of value).

In the processing industry (with an employment of 300 people) the output was 2 285 tonnes in 1995. The main product is canned anchovy.

Current and Prospective Assessment

Slovenia's production and foreign trade data, when compared to the corresponding EC figures, are quite low and therefore they should not have a significant impact upon the Community as a whole.

It will be necessary for Slovenia to establish a fisheries administration which is capable of implementing the Common Fisheries Policy — in particular the management of resources, the keeping of a fishing fleet register, the application of structural policy for the sector, the management of the market scheme and the collection of all statistical data — as well as the EC's policies on health, hygiene and environmental matters.

Conclusion

The sector will most likely not represent a problem for accession.

Energy

Main EU energy policy objectives, as reflected in the Commission White Paper 'An energy policy for the EU' include enhancement of competitiveness, security of energy supplies and protection of the environment. Key elements of the energy *acquis* comprise of Treaty provisions and secondary legislation particularly concerning competition and state aids, internal energy market (including directives on electricity, price transparency, gas and electricity transit, hydrocarbons licensing, emergency response including security stock obligations, etc.), nuclear energy, as well as energy efficiency and environmental rules. Development of Trans-European Energy Networks and support for energy R & D are other important elements of energy policy. Ongoing developments include liberalisation of the gas sector, energy efficiency *acquis* and the Auto-oil programme.

In the field of nuclear energy, the Community *acquis* has evolved substantially from the original EAEC Treaty to a framework of legal and political instruments, including international agreements. At present, it addresses issues of health and safety, including radiation protection, safety of nuclear installations, management of radioactive waste, investment including Euratom financial instruments, promotion of research, nuclear common market, supplies, safeguards, and international relations.

The Europe Agreement provides for cooperation to develop the progressive integration of the energy markets in Europe and includes provi-

sions on assistance within the related policy areas.

The White Paper preparing CEECs for the internal energy market underlines the need for full application of key internal market directives in combination with EC competition law. As to the nuclear sector, the White Paper refers to nuclear supply safeguards and shipments of nuclear waste.

Descriptive Summary

Slovenia imports more than 70 % of its energy requirements, particularly oil and gas (30 and 10 % of the energy balance respectively), but also solids and nuclear fuels. Indigenous resources are essentially lignite (causing serious environmental pollution) and low quality subbituminous coal representing 20 % of the energy balance, but also some hydropower, biomass and uranium (mining stopped in 1990 and decommissioning is ongoing).

Mining of solid fuels will continue in future for strategic reasons, but production has already decreased sharply over the last years (lignite from 5,1 to 3,9 million tonnes in the period 1985-1995 and brown coal from 2,6 million tonnes to 1 million tonne in the period 1989-1995).

External dependency can be managed well thanks to a diversified geographical origin of imports and good network connections. The electricity grid is since 1974 interconnected with the Western European UCPTE network. Oil and gas are imported from Russia but also from other sources. Energy efficiency is only half of the EU average due to its heritage of the past: low prices, obsolete and inefficient technologies and inadequate energy efficiency policies.

One US Pressurised Water Reactor at Krsko supplies 20 % of the electricity needs in Slovenia and exports 50 % of its electricity to Croatia. This jointly Slovenia-Croatian owned nuclear plant is supervised by the Slovenian Nuclear Safety Administration within the Ministry of Environment and Physical Planning. Though not required by the *acquis*, an independent supervisory structure would be desirable. Slovenia should implement this principle included in the Nuclear Safety Convention recently ratified. Investments have been made to ensure that nuclear safety is maintained at a high level. The fact that this power plant is built on a fault line has led to further seismological analysis in its surroundings. One research reactor is in operation in Ljubljana.

Current and Prospective Assessment

The 1996 'Strategy for efficient energy use and supply in Slovenia' is in line with EC energy policy and includes: market orientation, security of energy supplies, protection of the environment and improvement of energy efficiency.

The competition framework in the energy sector is progressively approximating with the directives of the internal energy market in combination with the application of EU competition law. Adoption of specific energy laws should be stepped up.

Energy prices have been considerably increased, but certain prices are, for social or other reasons, still (cross)-subsidised and do not recover costs. Government policy is to increase prices by 7 % per annum (in real terms) and to be on ca. 80 % of average EU prices in the year 2000.

Energy companies are generally state dominated monopolies but there are some small independent power producers. For the management of public utilities in the sector, statutory legislation should be established to ensure efficient management of state owned enterprises and to avoid distortive competition. To ensure future competitiveness of the companies, real price increases should be in line with Government targets.

Current oil stocks (thirty days of consumption) do not comply with Community *acquis* on emergency preparedness foreseeing among others, 90 days of mandatory stocks. In the event of rapid adoption of legislation, the EC target could be reached in the medium term.

Restructuring of the solid fuels sector continues and its social and regional consequences will have to be addressed whereas the state interventions should be assessed against EC state aid rules.

Slovenia has started the development of Community conform efficiency legislation (e.g. labelling appliances, minimum efficiency norms) as well as environmental norms (e.g. fuel quality standards) but more remains to be done. In this context, it should be noted that invest-

ments in the Lendava refinery are needed in order to have a chance to compete on the already saturated European market.

Nuclear fuel, on the basis of Slovene uranium, was fabricated in the USA, where also the enrichment services were largely purchased. Spent fuel from reactors will be shipped back to the USA.

The common nuclear materials supply policy of security through diversification of sources will apply to Slovenia for supply contracts concluded after accession. From a long term supply perspective in an enlarged EU it would be desirable for Slovenia to procure at least part of its uranium needs on the basis of long term contracts.

Spent fuel from Krsko is stored in the plant pool and its capacity may be increased. Interim storage in dry casks could also be envisaged. Some of them could be stored in Croatia which benefits from the electricity produced at Krsko. However, the long term final disposal of spent fuel is not yet defined and should therefore be further analysed. The Government has started to collect funds for the decommissioning of the Krsko plant at the end of its operation.

Upon accession, Slovenia would need to comply with the provisions of the Euratom Treaty, in particular those related to supply of nuclear material, the nuclear common market, safeguards, health and safety and international agreements. The country has not yet adhered to or fully implemented all the relevant international regimes in these fields (*inter alia* Nuclear Suppliers Guidelines, IAEA extended reporting and accession to the Nuclear Energy Agency of the OECD) but has a full-scope safeguards agreement in force with the IAEA. No major difficulties in applying Community legislation in these areas are however expected. Specific attention should be given to the operation safety of the Nuclear Power Plant. The independence of the safety authority should be supported.

Conclusion

Provided that current efforts are maintained energetically, Slovenia should be in a position to comply with most of the EC energy legislation in the next few years. However, matters such as the adjustment of monopolies including import and export, access to networks, energy pricing, state interventions in the solid fuels, emergency preparedness including the building up of mandatory oil stocks and the development of energy efficiency and fuel quality standards need to closely followed.

No major difficulties are foreseen for compliance with Euratom provisions but Slovenia should adhere to, or implement fully, certain international nuclear agreements. Nuclear safety standards should be handled appropriately and longer term solutions for nuclear waste will have to be found.

Transport

Community transport policy consist of policies and initiatives in three fundamental areas:

☐ improving quality by developing integrated and competitive transport systems based on advanced technologies which also contribute to environmental and safety objectives;

☐ improving the functioning of the Single Market in order to promote efficiency, choice and user-friendly provision of transport services while safeguarding social standards;

☐ broadening the external dimension by improving transport links with third countries and fostering the access of EU operators to other transport markets (The Common Transport Policy Action programme, 1995-2000).

The Europe Agreement provides for the approximation of the legislation with Community law and cooperation aiming to restructure and modernise transport, the improvement of access to the transport market, the facilitation of transit and the achievement of operating standards comparable to those in the Community.

The White Paper focuses on measures for the accomplishment of internal market conditions in the transport sector, including such aspects as competition, legislative harmonisation and standards.

Descriptive Summary

Slovenia has traditionally been a transit route for traffic with Greece and Asia Minor; the infrastructure was developed accordingly. The political changes at the end of the 80s, together with the war in ex-Yugoslavia, led to a major reorientation of traffic flows, with a sharp fall in Northwest-Southeast traffic and a gradual rise in traffic on the Southwest-Northeast axis, with much of the latter using road infrastructure not built for such traffic volumes. The advent of peace should restore Slovenia's role as a transit route between Greece and the rest of the Union, and there may be some new constraints on infrastructure. Slovenia is in the middle of a major programme of investment in improvements to its road network, mainly at this stage on the Southwest-Northeast axis; it will also need to improve border crossing infrastructures to cope with growing demand for traffic to and from Croatia. As a transit country, the fact that land and sea borders with Croatia are not yet fully demarcated could eventually cause problems.

Current and Prospective Assessment

As regards completion of the internal market, Slovenia has made substantial progress towards adopting the *acquis* despite being the last country to conclude an association agreement with the EC. Slovenia's international transport sector already largely applies, or is well on the way to applying rules similar to the Union's, in particular in the air, maritime, combined transport, road passenger transport and road haulage fields. The absence of statutory legislation for state-owned companies hinders the establishment of a transparent market organisation. In the rail sector, care should be taken to ensure, in the coming years, effective application of the *acquis* in the public service aspects and standardisation of accounts. Slovenia should be able swiftly to integrate into the internal market for transport subject to alignment of its road tax system on the *acquis* in this field and an opening-up of the road haulage market.

The development of an integrated and competitive transport system is an objective of which the Slovenian authorities are aware; achieving an acceptable level of safety and optimal use of the transport system are likely to be the two main difficulties. Slovenia's progress on safety is satisfactory on the whole. In contrast, the objective of coherence in the transport system appears harder to attain. Slovenia is likely to face a steady rise in the share of road transport and will have to focus its efforts on the use of railways.

In order to improve links with the Member States and its neighbours, Slovenia is planning to invest about 2,2 billion ECU of its own budget over the period 1995-1999 in transport infrastructure used by international traffic, primarily on trans-European corridors. This sum amounts to about 2,9 % of GNP, a respectable figure.

Conclusion

Slovenia has made notable and rapid progress in the adoption of the *acquis* in the transport sector. Provided that it makes additional efforts on the operation of its road haulage market (in particular on market access and tax) and clarifies the financial procedures in the rail sector — measures which are perfectly achievable — the transport sector is unlikely to pose major problems as regards adoption of the internal market *acquis*.

It will be necessary to make sure, however, that the resources are available which are needed to lay the foundations for the future trans-European transport network extended to the applicant countries.

Small and Medium Enterprises

EU enterprise policy aims at encouraging a favourable environment for the development of SMEs throughout the EU, at improving their competitiveness and encouraging their Europeanisation and internationalisation. It is characterised by a high degree of subsidiarity. The complementary role of the Community is defined and implemented through a Multiannual Programme for SMEs in the EU. This programme provides the legal and budgetary basis for the Community's specific SME policy actions. The *acquis* has so far been limited to recommendations on specific areas, although legislation in other sectors also affects SMEs (e.g. competition, environment, company law).

The Europe Agreement provides for cooperation to develop and strengthen SMEs, in particular in the private sector, *inter alia* through provision of information and assistance on legal, administrative and tax conditions.

The White Paper contains no specific measures.

Descriptive Summary

Small and medium-sized enterprises constitute the large majority of the Slovene enterprise sector. Since 1988, individuals are allowed to set up their own private company (Law on Enterprises and Law on Crafts). The privatisation process, which is now in its final phase, has led to the break up of a number of larger industrial companies into medium-sized enterprises.

The Ministry of Economic Affairs has presented a strategy which, *inter alia*, foresees the decentralisation of SME development towards the local level. The Chamber of Economy and the Chamber of Crafts, with compulsory membership, are also present at local level.

The main policy measures include profit tax discounts for start-ups and small enterprises for the first four years and rebates for the import of foreign machines and raw materials (especially for export-oriented companies). Credit guarantees are arranged through a fund for SMEs and locally by municipal funds. Further, there are training and international promotion supports, and links with small business associations of neighbouring countries. These measures concern the companies with less than 50 employees since those are the companies classified as 'SMEs' in Slovenia.

Current and Prospective Assessment

The government recognises some weaknesses in its SME development policy, especially regarding the coherency and the coordination of the various action programmes. This situation should be improved in the years to come. Small and medium enterprises form an important innovation and export potential in Slovenia. With a view to supporting the development of a competitive enterprise sector enabling Slovenia to catch up with economic development in the EU these assets merit support.

The ongoing efforts to strengthen the SMEs during the pre-accession period will therefore need to be continued.

Conclusion

There are no specific problems foreseen regarding Slovenia's future participation in this sector

3.5. Economic and Social Cohesion

Employment and Social Affairs

Community social policy has been developed through a variety of instruments such as legal provisions, the European Social Fund and actions focused on specific issues, including public health, poverty and the disabled. The legal *acquis* covers health and safety at work, labour law and working conditions, equal opportunities for men and women, social security coordination for migrant workers and tobacco products. Social legislation in the Union has been characterised by laying down minimum standards. In addition, the social dialogue at European level is enshrined in the Treaty (Article 118b), and the Protocol on social policy refers to the consultation of the social partners and measures to facilitate the social dialogue.

The Europe Agreement provides for approximation of legislation with Community law and cooperation on improving standards of health and safety at work, labour market policies and the modernisation of the social security system.

The White Paper mentions measures for approximation in all the areas of the *acquis*.

Descriptive Summary

In Slovenia there are a number of trade unions, including four major ones. The employers are mainly represented by four organisations. At national level the tripartite *social dialogue* functions well. Further development of the social dialogue will be supported by the planned adoption of a new framework law on Labour Relations.

According to ILO methodology, the unemployment rate was 7,3 % in 1996. The Slovenian registered unemployment figures are higher but have an in-built tendency to overstate unemployment.

Slovenia has developed a regionalised employment service structure to handle active *labour market policy*.

Slovenia has the same type of financing problems in the area of *social security* that are encountered in most European countries. In 1994, the part of GDP spent on social security was similar, at 25 % of GDP, to that of many Member States. Unless the social insurance system is reformed, a widening deficit will strain the national budget in the near future. Some of the changes in the system, however, may increase the risk for some groups to fall through the net of social protection. Social assistance schemes as a means of last resort are rather poor. Continued efforts are required to ensure that measures of social protection are developed.

The overall situation of *public health* in Slovenia is comparable to EU levels.

Current and Prospective Assessment

In Slovenia, work on the approximation of *health* and *safety* legislation is still in an initial phase. Although no timetable has been indicated by Slovenia, the approximation process to the EU *acquis* is underway. Appropriate independence of the existing labour inspection structures in compliance with ILO Convention No 81 has to be guaranteed.

The main principles of European *labour law* have already been introduced into Slovenia's legal system. Some adaptations are still necessary concerning the protection of employees in case of a transfer of the undertaking and the setting-up of a guarantee institution to protect employees in the event of insolvency of their employer. Smaller amendments are needed concerning collective dismissals, the information of employees on the working conditions applicable to their work contract as well as concerning the existing working time regime. Even if there is already a system of works councils in force, the social dialogue on company level needs to be developed. A new labour code is being prepared to secure full compliance with the *acquis*. Generally, the continuation of policies to modernise the labour market should be encouraged.

The main provisions of EC legislation concerning the *equal treatment of men and women* are covered by the Slovene national legislation. Adaptation of the rules for parental leave is needed.

Concerning the right to the free movement of workers, there would appear to be no obstacles to prevent Slovenia from being able to implement the provisions of the *acquis* in this area. The introduction of the right to free movement will however require changes in the national law, particularly as regards access to employment and a treatment free from discrimination on grounds of nationality.

In the field of *social security for migrant workers*, accession does not, in principle, pose major problems, but certain technical adaptations will be necessary. More important is the administrative capacity to apply the detailed co-ordination rules in cooperation with other countries. Slovenia appears to have many of the administrative structures necessary to carry out these tasks, but further preparation and training will be necessary prior to accession.

The Directives on the *warning labelling of cigarette packages* and the *maximum tar content* have not yet been transposed into Slovene legislation.

Conclusion

In the social policy field, Slovenia has already taken a number of significant steps in preparation for its future EU membership. Social reforms should be continued and the social dialogue should be developed. If Slovenia persuades her efforts, she is likely to be able to take on the obligations of EU membership in the medium term.

Regional Policy and Cohesion

In accordance with Title XIV of the Treaty, the Community supports the strengthening of cohesion, mainly through the Structural Funds. Slovenia will have to implement these instruments effectively whilst respecting the principles, objectives and procedures which will be in place at the time of its accession.

The Europe Agreement provides for cooperation on regional development and spatial planning, notably through the exchange of information between local, regional and national authorities and the exchange of civil servants and experts.

The White Paper mentions no specific measures.

Descriptive Summary

Slovenia's aggregate GDP has registered positive growth rates since 1993 and was at some 59 % of the EU average in 1995. After having grown with an annual average of nearly 6 % from 1990 to 1995, figures suggest a declining trend of unemployment amounting to approximately 7 %.

The present legal basis for Slovenia's regional development initiatives is the law on 'Stimulation of Development in demographically Endangered Areas' adopted at the very end of 1990 which covers 61 % of the territory and 24,6 % of the population. According to this law, the State provides cofinancing of infrastructure development projects at local level including public services and soft loans for economic activities (SMEs).

Recently, a law on Regional Development Promotion has been submitted to the national Parliament defining three types of problem areas in line with current EU practices (1,2 and 5b) and a border zone within the 10 km area distance from the border (to participate in Interreg-PHARE programmes). This law also suggests the establishment of Regional Development Councils and the establishment of a comprehensive information system. Spatial planning is defined in the long and mid term plans under the responsibility of the local self government.

The Ministry of Economic Relations and Development is in charge of regional development, the Ministry of Environment and Physical Planning deals with spatial planning. Twelve functional planning regions were created but without elected representations or established administration. Since 1995 local administration is organised on the basis of 147 local authorities. The Law on Public Administration defines the competencies of these local bodies.

Slovenia's financial instruments at the disposal of regional development initiatives are limited. However, the share of development related expenditures which could constitute potential counterpart funds to EC structural policy cannot yet be determined. Therefore, Slovenia's cofinancement capacity cannot presently be evaluated with sufficient reliability.

Current and Prospective Assessment

A new law on regional development is under preparation and the Government decided in November 1996 to establish an inter-ministerial Task Force for the development of a national policy in this field.

However, ministerial responsibility for regional development policy and spatial planning is in need of strengthening. In addition, the institutional structure seems embryonic with low inter-ministerial co-ordination.

Nevertheless, a clear political awareness seems to prevail in Slovenia as to the need for a regional policy and the establishment of administrative and budgetary procedures able to channel the EU structural actions.

Conclusion

Slovenia is currently establishing a regional development policy adapted to its regional disparities. Given the small size of the country, Slovenia's regional policy should be formulated within the framework of its national development strategy. Although some provisions are still to be implemented, Slovenia's administrative capacity seems sufficient to implement integrated regional development programmes efficiently. Subject to these necessary modifications, Slovenia should, in the medium-term, be ready to apply the Community rules and channel the funds from the EC structural policies.

3.6. Quality of Life and Environment

Environment

The Community's environmental policy, derived from the Treaty, aims towards sustainability based on the integration of environmental protection into EU sectoral policies, preventive action, the polluter pays principle, fighting environmental damage at the source, and shared responsibility. The *acquis* comprises approximately 200 legal acts covering a wide range of matters, including water and air pollution, management of waste and chemicals, biotechnology, radiation protection, and nature protection.

Member States are required to ensure that an environmental impact assessment is carried out before development consent is granted for certain public and private projects.

The Europe Agreement stipulates that Slovenian development policies shall be guided by the principle of sustainable development and should fully incorporate environmental considerations. It also identifies environment as an area for bilateral cooperation, as well as for approximation of legislation to that of the Community.

The White Paper covers only a small part of the environmental *acquis*, namely product-related legislation, which is directly related to the free circulation of goods.

Descriptive Summary

There are no particular environmental hot spots in Slovenia. However, there are important, and in some cases growing, problems, mainly in water quality and waste management, but also in air and soil pollution.

Surface and ground water quality has deteriorated in recent years, because of waste water originating from agricultural run-off, discharge of untreated municipal and industrial waste water, and leakage from industrial and municipal waste disposal sites. The quality of drinking water is low and there is little treatment of waste water though Slovenia is considering the launching of action to improve the situation. Waste management is an area of growing concern; here problems derive from rapidly growing untreated industrial and municipal waste and leakage from unregulated waste dumps. Power plants and, increasingly, urban traffic are the main sources of air pollution, which is especially important in the Ljubljana area. Acid rain has recently become a major problem. Extensive use of fertilisers and pesticides in agriculture contributes to soil pollution. Slovenia has an extraordinarily rich bio-diversity, but its erosion causes concern.

Slovenia has a framework environmental legislation (Environmental Protection Act of 1993), whose objectives and principles aim at sustainable development. A legislative system is also in place for air and water pollution, but there is no legislation for waste management, although the Government has recently adopted an extensive strategy for this area. On the whole, secondary legislation on implementation and enforcement is lagging behind.

Financial resources allocated to the environmental sector are very limited, well below the EU average, and below the investment requirements as assessed by the Slovenian authorities for implementing their National Environmental Action Programme. Economic instruments include the ecological development fund and a system for fines and permits.

Current and Prospective Assessment

Slovenia's environmental legislation has begun moving into line with that of the EU, but gaps in sectoral and enforcement legislation remain and there is insufficient information on the degree of compliance of recent legislation. In addition, Slovenia does not seem to have structures ensuring the compatibility of environmental legislation and policies with those of the Union. Critical for progress in achieving formal compliance with the *acquis* will be the adoption in all environmental sectors of subsidiary legislation for implementation, fully compatible with existing framework legislation.

In terms of White Paper measures for environment (both Stage I and Stage II), Slovenian legislation is partially compatible in most areas, but gaps exist in waste management, chemical substances and noise emission legislation.

Current levels of substantive compliance are still below EC norms in key areas — industry and energy sector, municipal waste and hazardous waste. Slovenia's focus on water quality has led to a relative neglect of compliance with other parts of the Community *acquis*, including product related directives and waste directives. Environmental concerns in the agricultural sector have to be addressed. Particular attention should be given to the quick transposition of framework directives dealing with air, waste, water and the Integrated Pollution Prevention and Control (IPPC) directive, as well as the establishment of financing strategies for legislation in the water, air and waste sectors requiring major investments.

Key measures for significantly raising substantive compliance levels would include a major focus on raising enforcement levels, increasing the national budget for environmental investment, easing administrative and parliamentary bottle-necks in developing new legislation, and further developing economic instruments. The country's environmental accession strategy should include implementation timetables for meeting the EC environmental *acquis,* starting among others with implementation of the framework and IPPC directives mentioned above.

Conclusion

Full transposition of the environmental *acquis* in Slovenia can be expected in the medium-term, if current plans for new framework and secondary implementation legislation are realised and if the National Environmental Action Programme and environmental accession strategy are quickly adopted. However, effective compliance with a number of pieces of legislation (e.g. urban waste water treatment, drinking water, aspects of waste management and air pollution legislation) could be achieved only in the long term, and will require a significant increase in environmental investment, as well as a major effort to reinforce administrative capacity.

Consumer Protection

The Community *acquis* covers protection of economic interests of consumers (including control of misleading advertising, indication of prices, consumer credit, unfair contract terms, distance selling, package travel, sales away from business premises and timeshare property) as well as the general safety of goods and the specific sectors of cosmetics, textile names and toys.

The Europe Agreement provides for approximation of legislation with Community law and cooperation with a view to achieving full compatibility between the systems of consumer protection in Slovenia and the Community.

Stage I measures of the White Paper focus on improving product safety, including cosmetics, textile names and toys, and on the protection of the economic interests of consumers, notably measures on misleading advertising, consumer credit, unfair contract terms and indication of prices. Stage II measures relate to package travel, sales away from business premises and timeshare property. New EC legislation which has been adopted recently (distance selling) or will be adopted soon (comparative advertising, price indication) will also need to be taken into account.

Descriptive Summary

Although Slovenia does not yet have a Consumer Protection Act , a draft law has been discussed for several years by Parliament. In September 1996, the Government set up on an agency for Consumer Protection which up to now, however, seems to lack the necessary resources. The Ministry for Economic Relations and Development is overall responsible for the coordination of consumer policy. Together with the Slovene Consumers Association, the Ministry draws up the annual program of consumer protection to be adopted by the Slovene Government. Consumers are represented by the Slovene Consumers' Association which was founded in June 1990 as an independent non-government, non-profit organisation. Due to its strong role, other consumer movements have difficulties developing.

Current and Prospective Assessment

The draft Consumer Protection Act appears to be on good track to be agreed. But further amendments or new provisions would still be required to make Slovene legislation fully compatible with EC standards on consumer policy.

On the protection of economic interests of consumers, it appears that the indication of the price of products and misleading advertising will only partly be regulated by the Slovene draft Consumer Protection Act. While the provisions on 'special types of sale' are more protective for consumers than under the EC Directive, regulations on unfair contract terms need to be clarified. There are important gaps in the areas of consumer credit, package travel and timeshare property where there appears to be few legislative initiatives or no legislation at all.

The Slovene law on product safety appears to have limited coverage compared to EC rules, and the draft Consumer Protection Act is unlikely to include any new or wider provisions to protect consumers in this area. On cosmetics, the main problem with the expected new regulation for cosmetic products concern the definition of the product. New regulations in line with EC Directives are expected for textiles names and the safety of toys.

The development of a strong and independent consumer movement, sustained by public authorities, will need to accompany the introduction of the *acquis*.

Conclusion

In spite of the inadequate legal situation, the prospect for legislative developments in alignment with the EC *acquis* appears positive in the medium-term provided work continues. But efforts need to be made to realign national law with the EC *acquis*. Slovenia needs to agree urgently the draft Consumer Protection Act as well as a number of other amendments intended to strengthen consumer protection, notably on general product safety.

3.7. Justice and Home Affairs

Present Provisions

The Justice and Home Affairs (JHA) *acquis* principally derives from the framework for cooperation set out in Title VI (Article K) of the Treaty on European Union (TEU), 'the third pillar', although certain 'first pillar' (EC Treaty) provisions and legislative measures are also closely linked.

The EU JHA framework primarily covers: asylum; control of external borders and immigration; customs cooperation and police cooperation against serious crime, including drug trafficking; and judicial cooperation on criminal and civil matters. The TEU stipulates key principles upon which such cooperation is based, notably the European Convention on Human Rights and the 1951 Geneva Convention on the Status of Refugees. It is also based implicitly on a range of international conventions concerning its fields of interest, notably those of the Council of Europe, the United Nations and the Hague Conference.

The legislative content of 'third pillar' *acquis* is different from the 'first pillar'; it consists of conventions, joint actions, joint positions and resolutions, (including the agreed elements of draft instruments which are in negotiation). A number of EU conventions (including the 1990

Dublin Convention, and conventions relating to extradition, fraud and Europol) have been agreed by the Council and are now in the process of ratification by national Parliaments; several other conventions, including one on external frontiers are in various stages of negotiation in the Council. The JHA *acquis* involves a high degree of practical cooperation, as well as legislation and its effective implementation.

The New Treaty

For many of the above matters, the entry into force of the Treaty resulting from the Amsterdam Inter-Governmental Conference will mark the end of the current cooperation framework.

Reiterating the objective of developing the Union into an 'area of freedom, security and justice', the new Treaty brings these matters, including the free movement of persons, asylum and immigration, into the Community's sphere of competence.

On the free movement of persons in particular, the new Treaty provides for the incorporation of the Schengen *acquis* into the framework of the European Union and binds any candidate for EU membership to accept that *acquis* in full.

With regard to matters remaining within the cooperation framework, i.e. policing and criminal justice, the new Treaty provides for the reinforcement of the cooperation system.

The Europe Agreement and the White Paper

The Europe Agreement includes provision for cooperation in the fight against drug abuse and money laundering.

The White Paper does not deal directly with 'third pillar' subjects, but reference is made to 'first pillar' matters such as money laundering and freedom of movement of persons which are closely related to Justice and Home Affairs considerations. Reference is also made to the Brussels and Rome Conventions.

Descriptive Summary

General Preconditions for JHA Cooperation

Slovenia joined the Council of Europe in 1993 and has ratified the most important instruments concerning human rights. The Constitution provides for an independent judiciary according to the rule of law.

Institutional reform of JHA institutions is well under way, although there is some concern about the efficiency and effectiveness of the judiciary. The Constitution guarantees data protection, in line with EU requirements, and Slovenia has ratified the 1990 data protection convention. A new law is in preparation, designed to modernise the data protection system, (see also separate section on the Single Market).

Asylum

Slovenia is party to the Geneva Convention and 1967 Protocol. Currently asylum law is regulated by the general Law on Foreigners, but a new asylum law, in line with EU requirements and covering social support as well as application procedures, is in preparation. Very few applications for asylum have been made. However, there are some 8 000 temporary refugees from former Yugoslavia, who have been granted temporary protection. A law on temporary refuge was adopted by the Slovenian Parliament in April 1997.

Immigration and Border Control

Some 190 million border crossings were made in 1995; of these some 4 200 were revealed to be illegal. Migrants are coming from Romania, Sri Lanka, Turkey and China. Slovenia follows the EU list of third countries for which visas are required and uses the EU standard visa format. Residence and immigration issues relating to aliens are covered by the 1991 Law on Foreigners. Readmission agreements are in place with Austria, Benelux, France, Greece Hungary, Croatia, Switzerland, Slovakia, Romania and Canada. Border management is thorough and effective.

Police Cooperation

Organised crime exists in Slovenia in the fields of arms trafficking, trafficking in women, prostitution, money laundering, vehicle theft, and smuggling of drugs. Legislation has been strengthened to help tackle organised crime more effectively, with specialist units being established; their level of experience is limited but their effectiveness is growing. Slovenia has signed the 1990 Money Laundering Convention, (see also separate section on the Single Market). Slovenia experienced isolated incidents of political terrorism at the end of the independence war, but there have been no recent incidents. Slovenia is concerned about the use of its soil by international terrorists. It is not party to the key international terrorist conventions, but domestic criminal Law covers terrorist activity.

Drugs

Slovenia is a major transit country for drug trafficking. Significant quantities of heroin have been seized in recent years. Domestic demand is increasing. Slovenia has acceded to the main international drugs conventions. Domestic legal measures to tackle drugs investigations are in place and there are special drugs units in the enforcement agencies.

Judicial Cooperation

Slovenia has ratified the main criminal conventions and has in place domestic legal procedures relating to cooperation on criminal matters. It is party to a number of Hague conventions and is developing its implementation capacities on the civil side as well. Generally the Slovene judiciary and wider legal system is inexperienced and inefficient and needs reform and human resource development to enable it to operate effectively.

Current and Prospective Assessment

There are still some gaps to be filled in Slovenia's legislation but for the most part the legislation is either in preparation or in place. Prio-

rities for the near future will be filling the remaining gaps with regards to international conventions, particularly in the criminal field and to develop the judicial system and institutions dealing with organised crime. In the migration field it will be important to develop and implement the new asylum law in a manner which respects the EU *acquis in full*.

Conclusion

For the most part Slovenia has demonstrated its capacity to make progress on key JHA issues, notably immigration and border control. Assuming progress is made on other issues, especially with regard to the judiciary and the full adoption of the asylum *acquis*, and systems to tackle organised crime are developed further, Slovenia should be able to meet the justice and home affairs *acquis* (present and future) within the next few years.

3.8. External Policies

Trade and International Economic Relations

The *acquis* in this field is made up principally of the Community's multilateral and bilateral commercial policy commitments, and its autonomous commercial defence instruments.

The Europe Agreement includes provisions in several areas requiring parties to act in accordance with WTO/ GATT principles, or other relevant international obligations.

The White Paper includes no provisions in this field.

Descriptive Summary

Slovenia has developed an open, trading economy and is a member of the World Trade Organisation (WTO). Upon accession Slovenia would have to comply with the obligations of the multilateral WTO agreements to which the Community is a party.

At present Slovenia maintains quantitative restrictions on the import of textile and clothing products. On accession Slovenia would have to apply Community quotas on quantitative restrictions. The Slovenian authorities are committed to phasing out these restrictions, with their elimination planned by 2005. On accession the Community textiles policy of the Community would be extended to Slovenia; any Community restrictions still maintained at the date of accession would require adjustment by an appropriate amount to take account of Slovenian accession.

Current and Prospective Assessment

On accession Slovenia would have to apply the Community's Common Customs Tariff, and the external trade provisions of the Common Agricultural Policy. The post Uruguay Round weighted average levels of most favoured nation duties for industrial products will be 10,9 % for Slovenia and 3,6 % for the Community.

In its relations with international organisations Slovenia should ensure that its actions and commitments respect the Europe Agreement and ensure a harmonious adoption of its future obligations as a member of the Community.

On accession Slovenia would become party to the Community's various preferential agreements. Preferential agreements between Slovenia and third countries would, in general, have to be terminated on accession.

In the area of trade in services and establishment Slovenia has sought to ensure that its multilateral commitments under the GATS are as consistent as possible with those of the Community; Slovenia has indicated its willingness to resolve any significant inconsistencies which may nonetheless come to light.

On accession Slovenia would have to repeal national legislation in the field of commercial defence instruments, and EC legislation would become applicable there.

Experience from previous accessions has shown that the automatic extension of existing anti-dumping measures to new Member States prompts third countries to raise problems in terms of the compatibility of this approach with relevant WTO provisions. It has also shown that

accession creates a potential for circumventing measures adopted by the Community under the commercial defence instruments. This happens when, prior to accession, substantial quantities of the products subject to measures are exported to the territory of the future Member State and, on accession, are automatically released for free circulation in the enlarged customs territory. These two problems would have to be addressed during Slovenia's pre-accession phase.

Slovenia is party to one of the four existing regimes for the non-proliferation of weapons of mass destruction, and is ratifying a second. Dual-use items are not currently subject to export control under Slovenian legislation. Arms export is controlled. It is questionable whether Slovenia would be able to abide by EC legislation upon accession since effective controls need time to be implemented. Slovenia should address this issue as a matter of urgency.

Conclusion

Slovenia is well placed to be able to meet Community requirements in this field within the next few years provided, in particular, that the question of the need for export controls on dual-use goods, is dealt with rapidly.

Development

The *acquis* in the development sector is made up principally of the Lomé Convention, which runs until early 2000.

Neither the Europe Agreement or the White Paper include provisions in this field.

Descriptive Summary

Slovenia has no preferential trade agreements with ACP countries, and no GSP schemes apply. No duty free access is granted by Slovenia.

Slovenia has no budget for development aid, although it has contributed financially to the reconstruction of Bosnia and Herzegovina.

Current and Prospective Assessment

On accession, Slovenia should apply its preferential trade regime to the ACP States and participate, together with the other Member States, in financing the European Development Fund (EDF), which provides financial aid under the Lomé Convention.

Slovenia could confront some difficulties in applying the present Lomé trade regime integrally from the date of accession.

Normally, new Member States accede to the Lomé Convention by means of a protocol on the date of their accession to the EU.

Conclusion

Slovenia will need to make significant progress if it is to meet EU requirements in this field within the next few years.

Customs

The *acquis* in this sector is the Community Customs Code and its implementing provisions; the EC's Combined Nomenclature; the Common Customs Tariff including trade preferences, tariff quotas and tariff suspensions; and other customs-related legislation outside the scope of the customs code.

The Europe Agreement covers the establishment of a free trade area with the Community and the progressive removal of customs duties on a wide range of products, according to clear timetables starting from the date of entry into force of the agreement.

The White Paper includes in Stage I, measures to consolidate and streamline the free trade established under the Europe Agreement, including legislation compatible with the Customs Code, Combined Nomenclature, etc. Stage II concerns the adoption of the full Community legislation, with a view to joining the customs union upon accession.

Descriptive Summary

On accession the Slovenian customs authorities would be required to assume all the responsibilities necessary for the protection and control of their part of the EU's external border. Besides the provisions on indirect taxation, they would be responsible for the implementation and enforcement at the external border of the Community's common commercial policy, the common agricultural policy, the common fisheries policy, etc.

Slovenia's capacity fully to apply the *acquis* presupposes the possibility to adopt and implement the Community legislation; and the existence of an adequate level of infrastructure and equipment, in particular in terms of computerisation and investigation means and the establishment of an efficient customs organisation with a sufficient number of qualified and motivated staff showing a high degree of integrity.

With the support of the technical assistance provided by customs programmes, Slovenia has achieved the adoption and entry into force on 1 January 1996 of a customs code compatible with the Community's customs code and its implementing provisions. The legislation on customs reliefs is in great measure compatible with the Community legislation, but important delays exist for counterfeit and pirated goods.

Slovenia is undertaking a continuous process of aligning its national goods nomenclature to the Community's Combined Nomenclature. A Slovenian Integrated Tariff already exists. This will greatly facilitate the comparison of the Slovenian tariff rates with those of the Commission Customs Tariff.

Slovenia adopted on 1 January 1997 the new system of cumulation of origin between European countries.

Slovenia has applied to become a contracting party to the EC/EFTA Common Transit Convention and the Single Administrative Document Convention. Slovenia has also applied to participate in one of the customs databases (TARIC).

Current and Prospective Assessment

Tax-free shops at land borders are allowed by Slovenia under national legislation although the Slovenian authorities intend to comply with the Customs Cooperation Council Recommendation of 16 June 1960 by 1 July 1998 at the latest. These tax-free shops are not allowed at land borders by the Recommendation nor are they permitted inside the EC territory, therefore the abolition of this kind of facility will be a condition for accession. However, the Slovenian authorities should accelerate the dismantling of these shops as soon as possible.

It will be important that the Slovenian customs authorities can participate appropriately in the various computerised systems necessary for the management, in the customs union/internal market, of the customs and indirect tax provisions, as well as the computerised systems for mutual administrative assistance in customs, agricultural and indirect tax matters. Computerisation is at a preliminary stage of development in Slovenia and will need to be upgraded.

Slovenia would need on accession to dismantle customs controls at the borders with EU Member States and with other acceding countries. The resources needed for the reinforcement of the border posts along its frontiers with non-EU Member States should be taken into account in its strategic planning.

Conclusion

If Slovenia continues major efforts to align its organisation and staff to the duties that have to be carried out by a modern customs administration, it should be able to meet EC requirements in the next few years.

Common Foreign and Security Policy

Following the declaration of independence on 25 June 1991, Slovenia has orientated its foreign and security policy towards the EU and NATO. Since it began participating in the political dialogue between the EU and the associated countries, Slovenia has been actively involved in the arrangements provided for under the Union's Common Foreign and Security Policy and whenever invited has supported EU actions within that framework. Slovenia is a member of the UN, OSCE, Council of Europe and many other international organisations. It is an associate partner of WEU, participates in the NACC, the PfP and has made clear its desire to become a member of the WEU and NATO as soon as possible. It has provided transit facilities for international forces en route to peacekeeping operations in former Yugoslavia; although it did not send troops to participate in IFOR, it has provided helicopters and medical equipment. Slovenia

also participates in a number of regional organisations including CEFTA and the CEI.

There are no territorial disputes between Slovenia and any member or associated State of the Union. There remain some problems, however, between Slovenia and Croatia, the most difficult of which is the dispute over the maritime border in Piran Bay. Other disputes concern the less contentious demarcation of land frontiers; property law; management of the Krsko Nuclear Plant; and banking claims. There are also a number of outstanding economic cooperation issues to be resolved with Croatia. Slovenia is concerned to ensure protection for the Slovene minorities in Italy and Austria.

Slovenia has a new and small diplomatic staff with limited experience and resources. In due course, it should nevertheless be able to play a full role as a member of the Union. It maintains 36 representations abroad and employs 108 diplomatic staff.

Slovenia does not formally participate in the control regimes concerning weapons of mass destruction but has established contacts with the relevant organisations and has stated its intention of participating in all relevant international arms control treaties. The small Slovenian armed forces, which are under democratic control, are being reorganised to meet NATO requirements. There is little defence industrial capacity. Slovenia is currently studying EU regulations with regard to export controls of dual use technology with a view to introducing the necessary legislation.

In its statement accompanying its application for membership of the Union, the Slovenian Government confirmed that it was ready and able to participate fully and actively in the Common Foreign and Security Policy.

The assessment of Slovenian foreign and security policy to date leads to the expectation that as a member it could fulfil its obligations in this field.

3.9. Financial Questions

Financial Control

The implementation of Community policies, especially for agriculture and the Structural Funds, requires efficient management and control systems for public expenditure, with provisions to fight fraud. Approximation of legislation is moreover needed to allow the system of 'own resources' to be introduced, with satisfactory provision for accounting.

The Europe Agreement contains no specific provisions on financial control. However it provides for cooperation in audit, including technical assistance from the Community as appropriate.

The White Paper includes no measures in this field.

Descriptive Summary

At the time of independence the audit and control of the economic sector was carried out by the self-managed institution, the Agency for Payments and Control (SDK), deriving from the Yugoslav system. The SDK carried out its function effectively within the Yugoslav economic system. Since independence Slovenia has had to progressively remove the powers of the SDK, and to transfer them to free market oriented institutions.

In terms of external control, the National Court of Audit, created in July 1994 and operating from January 1995, is the supreme control body of the State exercising control over government accounts, the state budget and resources extended for public purposes. The Court of Audit is empowered to supervise the collection of public duties and taxes, and to control the business operations of public and also private law entities and enterprises as far as they receive public funds from the state budget, and of other entities in which the State holds an interest. Its independence is guaranteed by the Constitution. Reporting generally follows international audit standards. Annual reports comprise summary information on findings, infringements and the balance of the use of funds, and may include recommendations for penal proceedings or investigations.

A special parliamentary Committee on control of finances and budget exercises a political control on the financial management of the Government.

In terms of internal control, the Department for Budget Inspection located in the Ministry of Finance verifies the various budget users' financial, material and accounting management according to an annual audit programme enforced by the Government. It covers regularity, legality and purpose of use. A preventive budgetary control is also secured by the Department of Public Accounting within the Ministry of Finance, and to some extent within each ministry.

Three bodies are responsible for cooperating with other countries in the fight against fraud, depending on the nature of a case: for criminal offences, the Criminal Investigation Service of the Ministry of the Interior within Interpol, for violations of customs regulations, the Customs Directorate of the Ministry of Finance, and for financial operations, the Office for Money Laundering Prevention. State revenues tax control is carried out by the Tax Services which perform tax monitoring.

Current and Prospective Assessment

Following independence, international standards of financial management and control were introduced in line with practice in EU Member States. Several EU Regulations are applicable from the date of ratification of the Europe Agreement, targeting at good governance and the protection of the Community interests in sound management of Community funds. While legislation generally reflecting the *acquis* in the field of financial control has been adopted or is in the process of adoption, implementation and enforcement structures need to be developed and strengthened.

There is no central authority responsible for fighting against fraud, nor is such a body envisaged. Internal and external control bodies have not yet reached the level of efficiency to be compatible with EU practice and standards.

The customs internal control is not a specific audit platform for 'own resources' and further cooperation with the Commission will be required to establish whether accounting procedures entirely fulfil the requirements of Regulation (EEC) No 1552/89.

The actual reporting and follow-up procedures suffer from an unsatisfactory conceptual definition of the Courts Role on the one hand and excessive formalisation on the other. The actual situation is due to a great extent to the lack of clearly established audit concept as well as the lack of well trained staff.

The National Court of Audit needs to be strengthened in order to carry out performance and project audits including a revision of the reporting system. The Ministry of Finance also requires additional resources to carry out tasks effectively.

In the agricultural sphere, a distinction should be made between ex-ante and ex-post control. Accounting procedures, control criteria and the framework of administrative sanctions in the event of irregularity should be clarified.

Given the absence of a regional policy comparable to that of EU Member States, it is difficult to provide any assessment of the financial control tools in the field of regional development and regional development funding. Efficient monitoring, control and audit structures would need to be set up in this area as well as in other areas covered by the structural funds.

Conclusion

Continued efforts are necessary to strengthen financial control and audit functions.

Budgetary Implications

The communication entitled 'Agenda 2000' sets out the overall financial framework which should accommodate the budget impact of any future enlargements in the medium term. This is to ensure that any enlargement is compatible with proposed Community policy guidelines within reasonable budget limits.

As things stand, it would be difficult, not to say premature, to attempt precise country-by-country evaluations of the budgetary implications of each of the applicants joining the Union. Exactly what the impact would be may vary considerably depending on a whole series of factors:

☐ the date on which the applicant country joins;

☐ developments in Community policies between now and then, in particular the decisions to be taken on further reform of the common agricultural policy and new guidelines for structural measures;

☐ the progress made by the applicant countries in terms of growth, increasing their competitiveness and productivity and their ability to absorb the *acquis*;

☐ the transitional measures that will come out of the negotiations.

Only a few orders of magnitude for certain budget categories and an overall estimate can be given purely as a guide.

Expenditure

If the common agricultural policy were to be reformed along the lines suggested by the Commission, once the reforms were fully up and running and in terms of just market intervention measures, Slovenia's accession would give rise to only marginal additional expenditure in relation to likely expenditure on the present fifteen Member States.

Application of the other internal Community policies in the new member countries would be likely to involve additional expenditure probably in excess of their relative proportion of Union GNP, since for certain policies the additional implementing costs also depend on the target population, the geographical area covered or the number of Member States involved in the coordination and harmonisation measures. The GNP of Slovenia is currently 0,3 % of total Union GNP.

By contrast, Slovenia's accession should not involve significant additional expenditure as far as Union external action is concerned.

It should not be forgotten that when an applicant country joins, the Community budget will no longer have to bear the costs of grants the country was eligible for under the various pre-accession programmes, such as PHARE.

In light of the above, the estimated costs in the three areas mentioned arising from Slovenia's accession should fall within the range of, annually, *1 to 1,3 billion ECU* in 2005/2006 (at constant 1997 prices).

Revenue

Assuming full application of the own resources system, the new members' contributions to the Community budget should, in terms of total GNP and VAT resources (taking account of the capping rules applying to VAT), be close to the proportion of the Union's GNP they account for, which in Slovenia's case is 0,3 %. Slovenia's portion of traditional own resources will depend on the structure of its trade flows at the time of accession.

To ensure that the own resources are established, monitored and made available in line with Community regulations, Slovenia will have to overhaul its current customs system. In addition, for the purposes of accurately calculating the GNP resource considerable improvements will have to be made to the national accounts to ensure that they are reliable, homogeneous and complete. Improving the statistics will also be essential for drawing up the VAT own resources base, which will mean bringing Slovenia's VAT system fully into line with the Community directives.

4. Administrative Capacity to apply the *Acquis*

The European Council in Madrid in December 1995 concluded that the harmonious integration into the EU of the Central and Eastern European applicant States would, in particular, require the adjustment of their administrative structures. This chapter examines the current state of the public administration in Slovenia, including relevant aspects of the judicial system, and assesses the current and prospective ability to carry out the functions required of it in a modern, democratic state, with a particular focus on the need to administer matters related to the *acquis*.

4.1. Administrative Structures

A description of Slovene constitutional structures, their powers and responsibilities, including those of local government, is given in Chapter 1.

At the central level there are 15 ministries, in addition to the Prime Minister's Office and a number of additional ministers without portfolio. For the handling of specific issues inter-ministerial committees can be established, at the level of ministers or state secretaries.

As yet, there is no full statutory basis for a Civil Service, nor any clearly stated set of principles governing the role of the Civil Service. Instead, administrative procedures legislation governs the work which the Civil Service undertakes. A Civil Service Act is under preparation.

The civil service is politically independent. Non-career civil servants may be appointed into State Secretary posts. Senior members of a political party are not permitted to fill civil service posts.

There are about 25 000 civil servants in the Slovene public administration. Overall, apart from specialised professions, pay levels in the public sector, while lower, are reasonably competitive with the private sector.

As a result of the Act on Ministries, the Ministry of Interior has been made responsible in 1995 for public administration and its reform. A reform programme has been submitted to the Slovene Government in June 1997, foreseen to be approved by the Government as part of the national pre-accession strategy before end 1997. The reform is based on an in-depth analysis of the Slovene situation and comprises the adoption of a new Civil Service Law in 1998. It is intended to be completed by end 1999. A state-secretary for administration has been nominated inside the Ministry of Interior to strengthen coordination, monitoring and implementation of the reform.

The Office of European Affairs supervises implementation of the White Paper (see also the section of the Introduction concerning relations between the European Union and Slovenia).

4.2. Administrative and Judicial Capacity

An important legacy of the past for the public administration of Slovenia has been the need, following independence in 1991, to transform the regional administration of Slovenia into one responsible for central government functions. While there was a continuity in personnel and administrative practice, the administration was largely under-equipped to perform all the additional functions.

The structures of the public administration are reasonably well adapted to the effective execution of its necessary responsibilities. In order to ensure that the positive development of the civil service over the last years is consolidated and reinforced it will be important to address the need for greater communication and cooperation within and between ministries; implementation and enforcement structures are at an early stage of development and will require significant additional efforts. There is a shortage of staff in the Slovene public administration, in particular in the area of the implementation and enforcement of legislation. This includes the judiciary.

In order to ensure a sound basis for the future positive development of the civil service in its proper role it will be important that a firm legal basis is established as soon as possible. The current arrangements go part of the way to meeting this requirement but are insufficient on their own.

The civil service is understaffed in a number of key departments. Although the civil service has expanded and continues to do so the intake of graduates is limited to a small base; there are serious shortages at middle and senior management levels. These problems will have important negative consequences for the ability of the civil service to function effectively, unless they are successfully addressed in the near future.

Public confidence in the civil service is variable. There is no evidence of significant corruption.

While there remains scope for improving efficiency and effectiveness of the administration, the administrative practice of coordination and cooperation is, nevertheless, developing, in particular against the background of the Slovene strategy to adoption EU policies and legislation. Professional levels are often good, but in order to provide a sound basis for continued European integration further development of administrative skills will be an important objective. There is still scope for improvement in skills at the level of general and financial management, and in the areas of policy analysis, monitoring and evaluation. Progress has been made in civil service training and plans are being developed for a civil service college. The Masterplan for the Implementation of Public Administration Reform in Slovenia (1997-1999) provides a comprehensive reform programme for which the Government is committed to make the necessary financial resources available. It will be important that decentralisation initiatives are carried through. Given the complexity of the reforms envisaged, its success will also depend on the strength of the policy implementation and coordination mechanism to be set up.

There is a need to extend coverage of the reform to the judicial system in Slovenia and to focus specifically on the EU internal market and its implementation and enforcement requirements. The success of the reforms, in particular in the EU area, will largely determine whether Slovenia will be able effectively to administer the *acquis*.

Key Areas for the Implementation of the *Acquis*

The uniform application of EC law: the effective application of the *acquis* presupposes that the judicial authorities of Member States are able to apply the provisions of the Treaty dealing with ensuring the unity and application of the *acquis*, and are able to ensure the proper functioning of the Single Market and Community policies in general. A high quality and well trained and resourced judiciary is necessary for the application by the courts of EC law, including cases of direct effect, and cases of referral to the European Court of Justice under the terms of Article 177 of the Treaty.

There is a particular need to train judges in Community commercial law. In addition, significant human resource constraints exist. However, if appropriate action is taken to develop the capacity of the judicial system, including in these respects, the system could be in a position, in the medium term, effectively to apply the *acquis*.

Single market: the ability of Slovenia to ensure the correct application of Community requirements in the Single Market, particularly concerning the free movement of goods and services presupposes the existence of highly developed and effective regulatory, standardisation, certification and supervisory authorities, able to act fully in accordance with EC rules. An analysis of these points is made in Chapter 3.1 (under 'The Four Freedoms').

Concerning the administrative capacity in respect of free movement of goods, the situation in Slovenia is largely satisfactory, although public procurement is an area of some concern. The Standards and Metrology Institute, a government linked body, is entrusted with both the standardisation and accreditation functions; Slovenia has yet to achieve the required separation between the regulatory, standardisation and product certification functions. Adequate structures and staffing for market surveillance will need to be established and developed in the competent public authorities for the ex-post control of product safety. Concerning the free movement of services the situation is much less satisfactory than for goods. The Financial Systems Department of the Ministry of Finance is concerned with all legislation and supervision in the field of private financial institutions. It is suffering from a shortage of experienced staff to deal with new legislation. The Bank Supervision Department, part of the Central Bank, has 36 staff. The Agency for the Securities Market lacks the legal base for enforcement; it has 15 staff. Supervision of the insurance sector is still in the early stages of development. The Insurance Supervisory Authority has 7 staff.

In order to meet EC requirements in this area staff shortages, in particular, must be addressed.

Competition: as explained in Chapter 3.1 (under 'Competition') enforcement of competition law requires the establishment of anti-trust and state aid monitoring authorities, and that the judicial system, the public administration and the relevant economic operators have a sufficient understanding of competition law and policy.

In Slovenia the central authority is the Bureau for the Protection of Competition which has 3 staff; this is inadequate. The level of expertise is not high. The ability effectively to implement EC requirements in this field will require considerable investment in human resources and the definition of the competences of the Bureau for the Protection of Competition. There is no state-aid authority, and the administrative arrangements in relation to state-owned enterprises (where there is a lack of suitable legislation) require attention; effective regulatory systems will need to be set up in order to ensure competition standards.

Telecommunications: in order to formulate and implement the many liberalisation regulations contained in the *acquis* in this field it is necessary to have a regulatory and policy making body that is effectively separated from any operating company.

In the Department for Post and Telecommunications 8 staff work on telecommunications. Further staff work elsewhere. The administrative capacity will need to be strengthened.

Indirect taxation: the effective administration of the indirect taxation *acquis* presupposes structures capable of implementing the EC legislation concerning the harmonisation of Valued Added Tax and excise duties in an environment in which fiscal controls at internal EU frontiers have been abolished; and the excise system is based on the tax warehouses, duty being payable at the local rate in the Member State at the time the goods are consumed. This requires a highly developed and well trained and resourced service, with a high degree of integrity.

In Slovenia the relevant authority is the Ministry of Finance (a central Ministry, 14 regional offices and 50 branch offices) with 3 200 staff. Due to a large turnover of staff, resulting partly from trained staff being recruited by the private sector, it is difficult to assess the capacities of existing staff. Some useful expertise is available. It will be necessary nonetheless to consolidate professional standards, including training measures and improvements in pay.

Agriculture: the administrative requirements in the agricultural area primarily concern veterinary and plant health control, to protect public health and ensure the free movement of agricultural goods; and the ability to administer the mechanisms and requirements of the CAP, including high standards of financial control and official statistics. These points are dealt with in Chapter 3.4 (under 'Agriculture'); general standards in the statistical field are examined in Chapter 3.3 (under 'Statistics').

Concerning the administrative capacity in respect of veterinary and plant health controls in Slovenia, various improvements will be required, including to the facilities and professional experience at border posts and veterinary laboratories. The overall staff of 93 at the Ministry of Agriculture (6 in the food sector) is very modest. The inspectorate for Agriculture, Forestry and Hunting has 124 staff and the Veterinary Inspectorate 116. Concerning the administration of CAP requirements, strengthening of the current administrative structures will be necessary.

In order to meet EC requirements in this area important improvements remain to be made.

Transport: the application of the EU internal market and competition requirements to the transport sector, the development of relevant infrastructure products, and other aspects of the transport *acquis* will present administrative challenges to new Member States.

The responsible government authority in Slovenia is the Ministry of Transport (96 staff). There is a shortage of qualified staff. The absence of statutory legislation for public enterprises involved in transportation could pose a problem for the *acquis*.

Employment and social policy: a central administrative requirement in respect of the *acquis* in this area is adequate inspection capacity, particularly concerning health and safety at work.

In Slovenia the Labour Inspectorate has 74 inspectors. It requires reinforcement of staff resources and expertise.

Regional policy and cohesion: the main administrative requirements in this area are the existence of appropriate and effective administrative bodies, and in particular a high degree of competence and integrity in the administration of Community funds.

In Slovenia the Ministry of Economic Relations and Development is in charge of regional development (59 staff, of which 2 are resposible for regional development; 5 work in the Regional Development Fund). The administrative arrangements in this area are at an early stage of development. The situation concerning financial control is not satisfactory (see the section, below, on 'Financial control'). The effective administration of the *acquis* in this area will require significant efforts to create an appropriate institutional, administrative and budgetary framework.

Environment: because EU environmental policy, involves the integration of environmental protection into EU sectoral policies the administrative requirement is potentially very wide, affecting many bodies not normally associated with environmental protection. However, the main responsibility lies with environment ministries and various subsidiary bodies.

In Slovenia the Environment Ministry employs 1 200 staff. Monitoring is carried out by the ministry and the sectoral authorities, enforcement by the National Inspectorate (28 inspectors). These arrangements are not yet adequate since only 40 % of inspectorate positions are filled. The effective administration of the *acquis* in this area will require training in inspection and enforcement procedures, and the areas of competence of the various actors needs to be clarified.

Consumer protection: in this area, the effective administration of the *acquis* requires the allocation of overall responsibility to a specific state body through which the formulation, implementation and enforcement of consumer policy and consumer protection legislation can be undertaken.

In Slovenia the governmental Ministry of Economic Relations and Development shares responsibility for consumer affairs with the semi-independent Office for Consumer Protection. There are 3 staff working on consumer protection. As regards non-governmental consumer bodies an already strong and independent consumer movement has developed. There remains confusion about the exact scope and objectives of consumer policy. This in part explains difficulties in the effective enforcement of consumer laws; however, other factors which need to be addressed include a lack of expert staff, organisational deficits, and a lack of sensitivity to consumer questions among the judiciary.

Justice and home affairs: oversight of justice and home affairs questions falls to the justice and interior ministries. The administrative structures need to be able to deal effectively with asylum and migration questions, border management, police cooperation and judicial cooperation. There is an overriding need for sufficient and properly trained staff with a high degree of integrity.

In Slovenia the justice and interior ministries are adequately staffed. The capacity to handle asylum and migration questions is not yet assured, since a new asylum-law — in line with EU requirements — is still being prepared, and currently very few applications for asylum have been made. Border management is adequate. Specialised police units have been established to combat organised crime, and they are generally effective. The judiciary is inexperienced and the judicial system inefficient; judicial cooperation is currently limited, but improving. The effective administration of the *acquis* in this area will require greater investment in the judiciary (in particular in human resource development, and training in EC law).

Customs: applying the *acquis* in this area requires an adequate level of infrastructure and equipment, including computerisation and investigation resources, and the establishment of an efficient customs organisation with a sufficient number of qualified and motivated staff showing a high degree of integrity.

In Slovenia the customs service employs 2 200 staff. Due to a high turnover of staff, it is difficult to estimate their efficiency, and therefore the adequacy of staffing levels. However, there are some positive developments to record.

Financial control: the protection of the Community's financial interests requires the development of anti-fraud services, training of specialised staff (investigators, magistrates) and the reinforcement of systems of specific cooperation. The implementation of Community policies, especially for agriculture and the Structural Funds, requires efficient management and control systems for public expenditure, with provisions to fight fraud. Administratively it is essential to have a clear separation between external and internal control. Police and judicial authorities need to be able effectively to handle complex transnational financial crime (including fraud, corruption and money laundering) which could affect the Community's financial interests.

In Slovenia there is no central authority responsible for fighting against fraud. The National Court of Audit is not yet in a position fully to perform its audit function. The Ministry of Finance has only 5 staff at the Department for Budget Inspection. The effective administration of the *acquis* in this area will require major efforts to strengthen the institutional structures.

4.3. General Evaluation

With comprehensive reform efforts it could be envisaged that the necessary administrative structures would be in place in Slovenia, in the medium term, effectively to administer the *acquis*.

If the necessary measures are taken, the Slovenian judicial system could be in a position, in the medium term, effectively to apply Community law.

C — Summary and Conclusion

Slovenia submitted its application for membership of the European Union on 10 June 1996. Its request is part of the historic process of ending the division of Europe and consolidating the establishment of democracy across the continent.

In accordance with the provisions of Article O of the Treaty, the Commission has, at the request of the Council, prepared an Opinion on Slovenia's request for membership.

Slovenia has not yet ratified the *Europe Agreement* signed on 10 June 1996. It must first modify its Constitution to remove the restrictions on ownership of property which still affect nationals of EU Member States. Slovenia's preparation for membership is therefore going ahead on the basis of the Interim Agreement which entered into force on 1 January 1997. The Government has put in place the necessary mechanisms to coordinate its policies for European integration.

The government has given particular attention to creating the institutional structures necessary to implement the *White Paper* of 1995 on the Single Market, a key element of the pre-accession strategy. The Government agreed in May 1996 a three year programme of transposition of these measures and plans to define an overall strategy on these issues before the end of 1997.

In preparing its Opinion, the Commission has applied the *criteria established at the Copenhagen European Council* of June 1993. The Conclusions of this Council stated that those candidate countries of Central and Eastern Europe who wish to do so shall become members of the Union if they meet the following conditions:

☐ stability of institutions guaranteeing democracy, the rule of law, human rights and respect for and protection of minorities;

☐ the existence of a functioning market economy, as well as the ability to cope with competitive pressures and market forces within the Union;

☐ the ability to take on the obligations of membership, including adherence to the aims of political, economic and monetary union.

A judgement on these three groups of criteria — political, economic, and the ability to take on the *acquis* — depends also on the capacity of a country's administrative and legal systems to put into effect the principles of democracy and the market economy and to apply and enforce the *acquis* in practice.

The *method* followed in preparing these Opinions has been to analyse the situation in each candidate country, looking forward to the medium term prospects, and taking into account progress accomplished and reforms already under way. For the political criteria, the Commission has analysed the current situation, going beyond a formal account of the institutions to examine how democracy and the rule of law operate in practice.

1) Political Criteria

The Slovene institutions function properly, with the different powers respecting the limits on their competencies and cooperating with each other. Elections in 1992 and 1996 were free and fair. The opposition plays a normal part in the operation of the institutions.

There are no major problems over respect for fundamental rights. Some improvements are still needed in the operation of the judicial system, and in restoring property to former owners dispossessed under the communist regime. The effectiveness of the fight against corruption needs further strengthening.

Slovenia therefore presents the characteristics of a democracy with stable institutions guaranteeing the rule of law, human rights and respect for and protection of minorities.

2) Economic Criteria

After a period of falling GDP, Slovenia has had positive growth since 1993 (5,3 % in 1994, 3,9 % in 1995, 3,1 % in 1996). This has been achieved in conditions of balance in public finances and external accounts, and falling inflation (9,1 % in

1996). Slovenia has 2 million inhabitants and GDP per capita is 59 % of the EU average. The agricultural sector employs nearly 7 % of the working population and contributes 5 % of gross value added. Trade relations with the EU have grown considerably since 1991 and now represent 65 % of Slovenia's external trade.

On the basis of its analysis, the Commission's judgement as to *Slovenia's ability to meet the economic criteria* established at Copenhagen is as follows.

Slovenia can be regarded as a *functioning market economy*. It has advanced considerably in liberalisation and privatisation, and achieved a successful stabilisation of the economy. However, there is a lack of competition in some sectors, in particular the financial sector, the working of the market mechanisms still needs some improvement, and the necessary reforms of the fiscal and social security systems are not yet completed.

Slovenia should be able to cope with *competitive pressure* and *market forces within the Union* in the medium term, provided that rigidities in the economy are reduced. It has a diverse export base, the workforce is skilled and highly trained, and infrastructure is relatively good. However, enterprise restructuring has been slow due to the consensual character of economic decision-making, and the incentives of workers and managers to preserve the status quo. Improvements in competitiveness have been hampered by rapid wage growth combined with low productivity growth. The low level of foreign direct investment reflects these structural problems, which need to be tackled.

3) Capacity to take on the Obligations of Membership

Slovenia's ability to take on the *acquis* has been evaluated according to a number of indicators:

☐ the obligations set out in the Europe Agreement, particularly those relating to the right of establishment, national treatment, free circulation of goods, intellectual property and public procurement;

☐ implementation of the measures set out in the White Paper as essential for establishing the Single Market;

☐ progressive transposition of the other parts of the *acquis*.

Slovenia, which has not yet ratified the Europe Agreement, has made some progress in applying the corresponding dispositions of the Interim Agreement, and has achieved a satisfactory rate of transposition of the rules and directives set out in the White Paper.

For most of the sectors related to the *Single Market*, and in particular on accounting, mutual recognition of professional qualifications and intellectual property, the legislative foundation is virtually in place. According to the Slovene authorities' own estimation, most of the necessary measures have been either partly or completely transposed. But further legislative effort will be needed to achieve full absorption of the *acquis*.

Notwithstanding the efforts which have been made, the progress made in transposing legislation still needs to be accompanied by concrete measures of implementation, as well as by the establishment of an effective administrative underpinning. Substantial work is still needed in the fields of public procurement, competition, insurance, freedom of capital movements, product comformity and standardisation. Introduction of VAT is a top priority. Implementation and application of legislation should be seen as essential elements of Slovenia's pre-accession strategy. Slovenia needs to go beyond primary legislation and cover also technical standards.

As for the *other parts of the acquis*, if it continues its efforts, Slovenia should not have particular difficulties in applying it in the medium term in the following fields: education training and youth; research and technical development; telecommunications; audio-visual; small and medium enterprises; consumer protection; international trade relations; development; and customs.

The current level and perspective for competitiveness of most of the Slovene *industry* enables a positive expectation on its capacity to cope with the competitive pressure and market forces within the Union in the medium term. There may however, be problems linked to certain labour market rigidities and for those sectors and companies, which have not yet undergone restructuring.

For the *environment*, very important efforts will be needed, including massive investment and strengthening of administrative capacity for enforcement of legislation. Full compliance with the *acquis* could only be expected in the long term and would necessitate increased levels of public expenditure.

Slovenia has already made satisfactory progress in the *transport* field. If it continues its efforts in road freight transport and the railway sector, transport should not pose difficulties for accession. Slovenia has undertaken to make the investments necessary to establish TENs in order to ensure effective functioning of the Single Market.

Slovenia should also be able to apply the acquis on *employment* and *social affairs* in the medium term. Efforts are still needed, however, on labour law and health and safety at work. Slovenia also needs to establish the autonomy of the labour inspectorate.

As for *regional policy* and *cohesion* Slovenia has adopted a development policy which should permit it in the medium term to implement Community rules and effectively use structural funds. But it will need to strengthen considerably its financial control mechanisms.

In *agriculture*, if progress is achieved on veterinary and phytosanitary controls, on strengthening the structures needed to apply the CAP, and on re-structuring the agrifood sector as well as on strengthening its rural development policy, membership should not create significant problems for Slovenia in the medium term in applying the CAP in an appropriate manner.

In *energy* efforts are still needed on monopoly operations, price fixing, access to networks and state intervention in the solid fuel sector. Slovenia has a nuclear power station at Krsko, which it shares with Croatia, and which produces 20 % of its electricity. It was built according to western technology. A solution needs to be found for its nuclear waste.

On the basis of the analysis of its capacity to apply the *acquis*, Slovenia could be in a position in the medium term to take and implement the measures necessary for removal of controls at its *borders* with Member States of the Union.

Slovenia's participation in the third stage of *Economic and Monetary Union*, which implies coordination of economic policy and the complete liberalisation of capital movements, could present some difficulties given the incompatibility of the rules governing the Central Bank with those of the EU, and also the need to restructure the banking sector. It is premature to judge whether Slovenia will be in a position, by the time of its accession, to participate in the euro area. That will depend on how far the success of its structural transformation enables it to achieve and sustain permanently the convergence criteria. These are, however, not a condition for membership.

Slovenia should be able to apply the *acquis* on *justice* and *home affairs* in the next few years, even if particular attention needs to be paid to the operation of the judicial system, treatment of asylum seekers and the fight against organised crime.

Slovenia should be able to fulfil its obligations in respect of the *common foreign* and *security policy*.

Since 1991, Slovenia has strengthened its relations with its neighbours and signed Friendship and Good Neighbourliness Treaties with them. There is, however, still a dispute with Croatia over maritime boundaries.

4) Administrative and Legal Capacity

If Slovenia undertakes substantial efforts to reform its administration, the necessary structures could be in place in the medium term to apply the *acquis* effectively.

The capacity of the judicial system to ensure correct and uniform application of Community law is important, particularly for achievement of the Single Market. In current circumstances it is difficult to judge Slovenia's progress in this field.

Conclusion

In the light of these considerations, the Commission concludes that:

☐ Slovenia presents the characteristics of a democracy, with stable institutions guaranteeing the rule of law, human rights and respect for and protection of minorities;

☐ Slovenia can be regarded as a functioning market economy and should be able to cope with competitive pressure and market forces within the Union in the medium term;

☐ Slovenia has to make considerable efforts to take on the *acquis*, particularly as regards the effective application in the area of the interna-

market. In addition, important progress will be necessary in the sector of environment, employment and social affairs and energy. More generally, further administrative reform will be indispensable if Slovenia is to have the structures to apply and enforce the *acquis* effectively.

In the light of these considerations, the Commission recommends that negotiations for accession should be opened with Slovenia.

The reinforced pre-accession strategy will help Slovenia to prepare itself better to meet the obligations of membership, and to take action to improve the shortcomings identified in the Opinions. The Commission will present a report no later than the end of 1998 on the progress Slovenia has achieved.

Annex

Composition of Parliament

Results of last general elections (November 1996)

Party	Abbreviation	Seats
Liberal Democrats	LDS	25
People's Party	SLS	19
Social Democrats	SDS	16
Christian Democrats	SKD	10
Single list Social Democrats	ZLSD	9
Pensioners	DeSUS	5
Nationalist	SNS	4
Other		

+ 2 MPs elected by the Italian and Hungarian communities.

Single Market: White Paper Measures

This table is based on information provided by the Slovenian authorities and confirmed by them as correct as at the end of June 1997. It does not indicate the Commission's agreement with their analysis. The table includes directives and regulations cited in the White Paper which total 899. These have been listed in accordance with the categorization used in the White Paper and in relation to the policy areas covered. The table shows the number of measures for which Slovenian authorities have notified the existence of adopted legislation having some degree of compatibility with the corresponding White Paper measures.

White Paper chapters		Directives		Regulations		Total
		Stage I	Stage II/III	Stage I	Stage II/III	
1. Free Movement of Capital	Slovenia	2	1	0	0	3
	Number of White Paper measures	3	1	0	0	4
2. FM and Safety of Industrial Products	Slovenia	18	40	0	0	58
	Number of White Paper measures	56	104	4	1	165
3. Competition	Slovenia	0	0	0	0	0
	Number of White Paper measures	*3	0	1	0	4
4. Social policy and action	Slovenia	9	2	0	2	13
	Number of White Paper measures	12	15	0	2	29
5. Agriculture	Slovenia	67	22	15	0	104
	Number of White Paper measures	93	46	62	2	203
6. Transport	Slovenia	17	11	7	8	43
	Number of White Paper measures	19	15	8	13	55
7. Audiovisual	Slovenia	1	0	0	0	1
	Number of White Paper measures	1	0	0	0	1
8. Environment	Slovenia	21	0	3	0	24
	Number of White Paper measures	31	7	7	0	45
9. Telecommunication	Slovenia	3	0	0	0	3
	Number of White Paper measures	9	7	0	0	16
10. Direct Taxation	Slovenia	2	1	0	0	3
	Number of White Paper measures	2	2	0	0	4
11. Free movement of goods	Slovenia	0	0	0	0	0
	Number of White Paper measures	0	0	0	0	0
12. Public Procurement	Slovenia	0	0	0	0	0
	Number of White Paper measures	5	1	0	0	6
13. Financial services	Slovenia	7	0	0	0	7
	Number of White Paper measures	13	8	0	0	21
14. Protection of personal data	Slovenia	0	1	0	0	1
	Number of White Paper measures	0	2	0	0	2
15. Company Law	Slovenia	1	3	0	1	5
	Number of White Paper measures	2	3	0	1	6
16. Accountancy	Slovenia	3	2	0	0	5
	Number of White Paper measures	3	2	0	0	5
17. Civil Law	Slovenia	0	0	0	0	0
	Number of White Paper measures	1	1	0	0	2
18. Mutual rec. of prof. Qual.	Slovenia	2	16	0	0	18
	Number of White Paper measures	2	16	0	0	18
19. Intellectual property	Slovenia	5	3	0	2	10
	Number of White Paper measures	5	3	0	3	11
20. Energy	Slovenia	5	0	0	0	5
	Number of White Paper measures	10	2	3	0	15
21. Customs law	Slovenia	0	0	5	105	110
	Number of White Paper measures	2	1	14	184	201
22. Indirect Taxation	Slovenia	0	0	0	0	0
	Number of White Paper measures	15	54	0	6	75
23. Consumer Protection	Slovenia	2	0	0	0	2
	Number of White Paper measures	8	3	0	0	11
Total	Slovenia	165	102	30	118	415
	Number of White Paper measures	295	293	99	212	899

Statistical Data

If not explicitly stated otherwise, data contained in this annex are collected from *Statistical Office of the Republic of Slovenia* (Statisticni Urad Republike Slovenije) with whom Eurostat and Member States' statistical offices are co-operating since several years in the framework of the PHARE programme. Regular data collection and dissemination are part of this co-operation process with the aim to enable the application of EU laws and practices in statistics. The data presented below have been compiled as far as possible using EU definitions and standards which in some cases differ from national practices. This may occasionally give rise to differences between the data presented here and those shown elsewhere in the opinion, which are generally based on the individual applicant countries' updated replies to the questionnaire sent to them in April 1996. The exact compatibility with EU standards on statistics and thus the comparability with EU figures can still not be guaranteed, particularly those statistics that have not been supplied through Eurostat, but have been delivered directly by the countries concerned. Wherever available, methodological notes are given describing content and particularities of statistical data presented in this annex. Data correspond to the information available as of May 1997.

Basic Data

	1990	1992	1993	1994	1995
	In 1 000 hectares				
Total area		2 025	2 025	2 025	2 025
Population (end of the period)	In 1 000				
Total				1 989	1 990.0
Females					1 022.9
Males					967.1
	Per 1 km^2				
Population density					98
	In % of total population				
Urban population				50.1	50.1
	Per 1 000 of population				
Deaths rate		9.7	10.0	9.7	9.5
Births rate		10.0	9.9	9.8	9.5
Income and GDP per capita	European Currency Unit				
Average monthly wage and salary per employee	709				731
GDP per capita	6 844				7 236
Structure of production: share of branch GVA	In % of total Gross Value Added				
Agriculture	5.5				5.0
Industry	36.9				32.1
Construction	4.8				5.0
Services	52.8				57.9

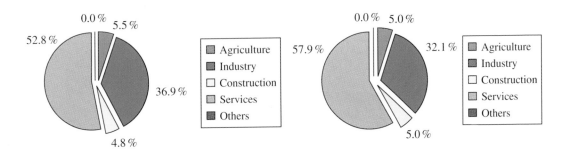

Share of branch GVA in 1990

0.0 % 5.5 %
52.8 %
36.9 %
4.8 %

Agriculture
Industry
Construction
Services
Others

Share of branch GVA in 1995

0.0 % 5.0 %
57.9 %
32.1 %
5.0 %

Agriculture
Industry
Construction
Services
Others

National Accounts

	1990	1991	1992	1993	1994	1995
	In millions of National Currency					
Gross Domestic Product (Current Prices)	196 762	349 408	1 017 965	1 435 095	1 845 831	2 202 021
	In billions of ECU					
Gross Domestic Product (Current Prices)		10.2	9.6	10.8	12.0	14.2
	In purchasing power standard per capita					
Gross Domestic Product				8 557.4	9 354.2	10 111.8
	% Change over the previous year					
Gross Domestic Product		− 8.9	− 5.5	2.8	5.3	3.9
Final consumption expenditure		− 8.4	− 3.1	11.4	4.0	5.9
of households and NPISH		− 11.0	− 3.6	13.6	4.6	7.0
of general government		− 1.7	5.3	5.3	2.1	2.5
Gross fixed capital formation		− 11.5	− 13.9	11.9	12.6	20.8
Exports of goods and services		− 20.1	− 23.5	0.6	10.5	0.7
Imports of goods and services		− 22.4	− 22.9	17.6	10.7	111.6
	In % of Gross Domestic Product					
Final consumption expenditure	70.6	73.8	75.5	79.6	77.3	78.1
of households and NPISH	53.2	54.8	55.1	58.5	57.0	57.7
of general government	17.4	19.0	20.3	21.1	20.1	20.4
Gross fixed capital formation	18.8	20.6	18.4	18.7	19.6	21.2
Exports of goods and services	90.8	83.5	63.1	58.8	59.1	54.7
Imports of goods and services	78.5	74.2	56.2	57.7	56.5	55.9

GDP (% Change over the previous year)

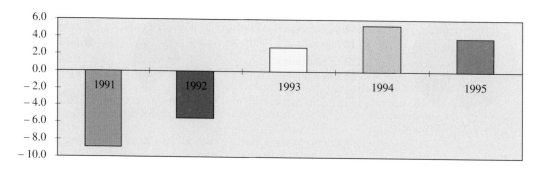

Main Economic Indicators

	1990	1991	1992	1993	1994	1995	1996
	Percentage change over the previous year						
Inflation rate RPI	549.7	117.7	201.3	32.3	19.8	12.6	9.7
	Previous year = 100						
Industrial production volume indices					106.4	102.0	101
Gross agricultural production volume indices				96.5	106.4	103.6	
Unemployment rate (ILO methodology)	In % labour force						
Total					9.0	7.4	7.3
Less then 25 years					22.2	18.8	18.8
25 years and more					7.1	5.6	5.6
	In billions of USD						
Gross Foreign debt		0.028	0.164	0.902	1.603	2.97	4.01
Balance of payments	In millions of USD						
Exports of goods			6 683	6 083	6 830	8 345	8 365
Imports of goods			− 5 892	− 6 237	− 7 168	− 9 298	− 9 218
Trade balance			791	− 154	− 338	− 953	− 853
Services, net			180	375	723	725	786
Income, net			− 91	− 51	108	147	89
Current account balance			926	192	540	− 36	46
Capital and fin. acc. (excl. reserves)			− 13	− 91	97	376	552
Reserve assets			− 633	− 111	− 642	− 220	− 587

Inflation rate: percentage change of yearly average over the previous year – all items index. Data refer to retail price index (official indicator of inflation rate in Slovenia).

Industrial production volume indices: industrial production covers mining and quarrying, manufacturing and electricity, gas and water supply (according to the NACE Classification Sections C, D, E). Index of industrial production covers enterprises with ten or more employees, except those engaged in the following activities: publishing, gas, steam and water supply.

Gross agricultural production volume indices: sliding average values of purchase prices in the last three years.

Unemployment rate (by ILO methodology): percentage of the unemployed in labour force. This rate is derived from LFSS (Labour Force Sample Survey) observing the following ILO definitions and recommendations.

Labour force: employed and unemployed persons in the sense of the ILO definitions stated below.

The employed: all persons aged 15+, who during the reference period worked at least one hour for wage or salary or other remuneration as employees, entrepreneurs, members of cooperatives or contributing family workers. Members of armed forces and women on child-care leave are included.

The unemployed: all persons aged 15+, who concurrently meet all three conditions of the ILO definition for being classified as the unemployed: a) have no work, b) are actively seeking a job and c) are ready to take up a job within a fortnight.

In Slovenia, LFSS excludes persons in compulsory military service and persons living in non-private households. Workers on lay-off and persons on maternity leave are classified among persons in employment.

Gross foreign debt: debt is extracted form the OECD's external debt statistics.

Balance of payments: data is derived from IMF database, their comparability with respective EU statistics can not be guaranteed, but balance of payments is compiled mainly in accordance to IMF standards. Balance in trade of goods in accordance with balance of payments principles. Exports and imports are both in fob values. Net income includes direct, portfolio and other investment income, compensation of employees. Current account balance by definition of *IMF 5th Manual*, capital transfers are excluded. Reserve assets: it means changes in reserve assets during the year; (+) signifies an increase, (−) a decrease in reserve assets.

Foreign Trade

	1992	1993	1994	1995	1996
Imports and exports (current prices)	In millions of USD				
Imports			7 304	9 492	9 397
Exports			6 828	8 316	8 306
Balance of trade			− 476	− 1 175	− 1 091
External trade volume indices	Previous year = 100				
Imports					
Exports					
Structure of Import by SITC (current prices)	In % of total import				
(0 + 1): food and live animals, beverage and tobacco			8.2	7.4	7.4
2: crude materials, inedible			6.5	6.5	5.1
3: mineral fuels and lubricants			7.1	6.6	7.9
4: animal and vegetable oils etc.			0.4	0.4	0.4
5: chemicals and related products			12.2	12.1	11.9
6: manufactured goods classified chiefly by material			19.4	19.8	19.7
7: machinery and transport equipment			31.8	33.8	33.7
8: miscellaneous manufactured articles			11.0	10.6	13.7
9: goods not elsewhere classified					
Structure of Export by SITC (current prices)	In % of total export				
(0 + 1): food and live animals, beverage and tobacco			4.8	3.8	4.0
2: crude materials, inedible			1.9	2.1	1.7
3: mineral fuels and lubricants			1.1	1.2	1.0
4: animal and vegetable oils etc.			0.1	0.1	0.1
5: chemicals and related products			10.3	10.5	10.6
6: manufactured goods classified chiefly by material			27.3	28.5	27.4
7: machinery and transport equipment			30.3	31.4	33.3
8: miscellaneous manufactured articles			24.0	22.2	21.9
9: goods not elsewhere classified					
External trade price indices	Previous year = 100				
Imports			102.1	116.3	
Exports			106.7	121.4	

Imports and exports (current prices) and structure of external trade by SITC (current prices): trade data exclude direct re-exports, trade in services and trade with customs free zones as well as licenses, know-how and patents. The data are based upon the special trade system. *Trade Classifications*: Slovenia introduced the Combined Nomenclature in 1996. Before that a national classification based on the Harmonised System was used. *Imports* are recorded on **CIF** basis and are captured with the date the commodities are released into circulation in the country. *Exports* are recorded on *FOB* basis and are captured with the date on which the commodities cross the customs border. The customs statistics is utilized for monitoring of foreign trade data. Eurostat has converted National Currencies to the US dollar by applying the International Monetary Fund annual average exchange rates.

External trade price indices: the indices are calculated from data for normal imports and exports without processing and without data regarding the countries of the former Yugoslavia.

Foreign Trade

	1992	1993		1994		1995		1996	
Structure of imports by main countries (current prices)		In % of total imports							
1st partner		D	25.0	D	23.7	D	23.2	D	21.7
2nd partner		I	16.2	I	17.2	I	17.0	I	16.9
3rd partner		HR	9.1	AT	10.3	AT	9.7	F	9.8
4th partner		AT	8.5	F	8.4	F	8.4	AT	8.8
5th partner		F	8.0	HR	6.8	HR	6.1	HR	6.2
Others			33.2		33.6		35.6		36.5
Structure of exports by main countries (current prices)		In % of total exports							
1st partner		D	29.5	D	30.3	D	30.2	D	30.6
2nd partner		I	12.4	I	13.5	I	14.6	I	13.3
3rd partner		HR	12.1	HR	10.8	HR	10.7	HR	10.3
4th partner		F	8.7	F	8.6	F	8.2	F	7.2
5th partner		AT	5.0	AT	5.5	AT	6.4	AT	6.6
Others			32.3		31.3		29.9		31.9

Structure of export by main partners in 1996

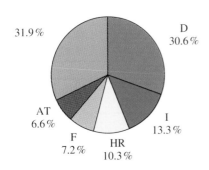

31.9%
D 30.6%
AT 6.6%
F 7.2%
HR 10.3%
I 13.3%

Structure of import by main partners in 1996

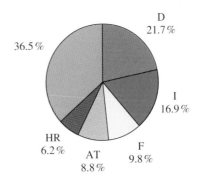

36.5%
D 21.7%
I 16.9%
F 9.8%
AT 8.8%
HR 6.2%

AT   Austria
D   Germany
F   France

HR   Croatia
I   Italy

Social Indicators

	1991	1992	1993	1994	1995
Population on 1 January	In thousand				
	1 999.95	1 998.9	1 994.2	1 989.41	1 989
Proportion of population by age 1 January 1995	In % of total population				
0-14 years					18.5
15-24 years					14.7
25-44 years					32.3
45-64 years					23.4
65 years and more					12.1
	Total number				
Live births	21 583	19 982	19 793	19 463	18 980
Deaths	19 324	19 333	20 012	19 359	18 968
Infant deaths					
Less than 1 year	178	177	134	126	
Still birth	106	110	93	105	
Marriages	8 173	9 119	9 022	8 313	
Divorces	1 828	1 966	1 962	1 923	
	Per 1 000 of population				
Crude marriage rate	4.08	4.57	4.59	4.18	4.2
Crude divorce rate	0.91	0.98	1.00	0.97	0.8
Natural growth	1.13	0.33	− 0.10	0.05	
Net migration	− 1.55	− 0.20	0.71	0.45	
Total population growth	− 0.42	0.12	0.61	0.50	
Total fertility rate	1.46	1.34	1.31	1.32	
Infant mortality rate	8.25	8.86	6.77	6.47	5.5
Late foetal mortality rate	4.89	5.47	4.68	5.37	
Life expectancy	At birth				
Males	69.54	69.45	69.40	69.6	
Females	77.38	77.25	77.29	77.4	
Life expectancy	At 65 years				
Males				13.3	
Females				16.8	

Labour Market

	1993	1994	1995	1996
		In % of population age +15		
Economic Activity Rate (ILO methodology)		57.6	58.7	57.6
		In thousand		
Average employment		851	882	878
Unemployment rate by age (ILO methodology)		In % of labour force		
Total		9.0	7.4	7.3
Less then 25 years		22.2	18.8	18.8
25 years and more		7.1	5.6	5.6
Registered unemployment (end of period)		In % of economically active population		
		14.2	14.5	14.4
Average paid employment indices by NACE classes		Previous year = 100		
Agriculture, hunting, forestry and fishing		83.3	90.1	100.1
Mining and quarrying		118.3	95.2	115.1
Manufacturing		95.0	106.5	95.2
Production and distribution of electricity, gas and water		79.7	144.9	95.0
Construction		101.7	94.3	103.7
Transport, storage and communication		92.2	97.2	98.2
Monthly nominal wages and salaries by NACE classes				
Agriculture, hunting, forestry and fishing				
Mining and quarrying				
Manufacturing				
Production and distribution of electricity, gas and water				
Construction				
Transport, storage and communication				
Monthly wages and salaries indices				
Nominal		125.4	118.4	115.3
Real		103.6	104.3	104.9

Economic activity rate (ILO Methodology): percentage of labor force in the total population aged 15+. This rate is derivated of LFSS (Labour Force Sample Survey) observing the following ILO definitions and recommendations.

Labour force: employed and unemployed persons in the sense of the ILO definitions stated below.

The employed: all persons aged 15+, who during the reference period worked at least one hour for wage or salary or other remuneration as employees, entrepreneurs, members of cooperatives or contributing family workers. Members of armed forces and women on child-care leave are included.

The unemployed: all persons aged 15+, who concurrently meet all three conditions of the ILO definition for being classified as the unemployed: a) have no work, b) are actively seeking a job and c) are ready to take up a job within a fortnight.

In Slovenia, LFSS excludes persons on compulsory military service and persons living in non-private households (so-called institutional population).

Unemployment rate (by ILO methodology): percentage of the unemployed in labour force. This rate is derived from LFSS (Labour Force Sample Survey) observing the following ILO definitions and recommendations (see ILO definitions above).

In Slovenia, LFSS excludes persons in compulsory military service and persons living in non-private households. Workers on lay-off and persons on maternity leave are classified among persons in employment.

Average employment, average paid employment indices by NACE classes: the data for entrepreneurial sphere cover enterprises and other organisations (private enterprises are included only if they have 3 or more persons in paid employment). Data come from the Labour Force Surveys. LFS data are therefore considered as annual data. The data cover also all budgetary, subsidised organisations and persons with secondary job are included. Armed forces, apprentices, employees on child-care and additional child-care leaves are excluded.

Registered unemployment (end of period): registered unemployment in percent — percentage of unemployed registered in civil economically active population, based on Labour force sample survey (LFSS). Registered unemployment data are based on the monthly administrative unemployment register.

Monthly wages and salaries indices: monthly *real* wages and salaries indices are derived from *gross* nominal wages and salaries indices divided by consumer price indices. The data for entrepreneurial sphere cover enterprises and other organisations (private enterprises are included only if they have 3 or more persons in paid employment). The earnings of external associates and consultants are not covered. The data cover also all budgetary, subsidised organisations and persons with secondary job are included. Armed forces, apprentices, employees on child-care and additional child-care leaves are excluded.

Public Finance

	1990	1991	1992	1993	1994	1995
Government budget	In billions of national currency					
Consolidated central government revenue						
Grants						
Consolidated central government expenditure				606.06	773.54	933.36
Consolidated general government expenditure						
Consolidated central government deficit/surplus				5.28	– 5.04	– 6.46
General government deficit/surplus						
Government budget	In % of Gross Domestic Product					
Consolidated central government expenditure				42.2	41.9	42.5
Consolidated general government expenditure						
Consolidated central government deficit/surplus				0.4	– 0.3	– 0.3
General government deficit/surplus						

Government budget: these data relate to central and general government as published in the IMF's *Government Finance Statistics Yearbook (1996) (GFSY)*; included also is the country's presentation in the *GFSY*.

Because the *GFSY* does not present statistics for general government, but for individual levels of government separately, the consolidated series presented here were obtained from central and local government data and adjusted in consolidation for the identified intergovernmental transfers.

Even though the statistics cover the central and local government published in *GFSY*, the coverage may not be exhaustive if some central or local government units are not included in that coverage. A measure of the exhaustiveness of the coverage can be obtained by comparing in the *GFSY* the note on the coverage of data for individual countries with the list of central and local government units provided.

It should be noted that the deficit/surplus used here is equal to revenue and grants minus expenditure, and does not take lending minus repayments into account (see further below).

The netting of inter-government transfers carried-out in the attached tables is limited to the current and capital transfers consisting of the identified grants and current and capital subsidies between the levels of government. Other types of transactions occurring between government levels, such as the payments of taxes and employers' social security contributions, and the reciprocal purchases of goods and services are not normally classified as inter-governmental transfers have not been eliminated in the consolidation process. Finally, whether the absence of data for current and capital transfers should be attributed to the absence of transfer or to lack of data is unclear; in all cases absence of information on transfers have been deemed to represent zero-transfers.

a) *Government expenditure* consists of general government cash expenditures on current and capital goods and services, interest payments and current and capital transfers but excludes non-cash transactions.

b) *Deficit/surplus* equals cash revenue and cash grants minus cash expenditure. This measure of the deficit/surplus differs from that used in *GFS* which equals cash revenue and cash grants, minus cash expenditure, minus net lending. This exclusion of net lending(consisting, in the *GFS* methodology, of operations in financial assets and liabilities carried out for specific policy purposes, rather than for liquidity purposes) brings the measure of the deficit/surplus presented here closer to the national accounts concept of net borrowing/net lending. Also, as a result of this exclusion, receipts from privatisation (classified as repayments in the *GFS* methodology) do not enter in the determination of the deficit/surplus presented in the attached tables (and therefore do not reduce the deficit).

Financial Sector

	1990	1991	1992	1993	1994	1995	1996
Monetary aggregates	In billions (10^9) of US dollars						
Monetary aggregate M1					1.35	1.62	1.66
Quasi money					4.45	5.84	6.34
	In billions (10^6) of US dollars						
Total reserves (gold excluded, end of period)				787.8	1 498.98	1 820.79	2 297.36
Average short term interest rates	% per annum						
Lending rate				49.61	39.42	24.84	19.30
Deposit rate				32.65	27.89	15.32	11.19
Official discount rate (end of period)					16.00	10.00	10.00
USD exchange rates	1 USD = ... SIT						
Average of period	27.57	81.29	113.24	128.81	118.52	135.36	
End of Period	56.69	98.70	131.84	126.46	125.99	141.48	
ECU exchange rates	1 ECU = ... SIT						
Average of period	34.164	105.523	132.604	153.222	155.025	179.213	
End of Period	76.017	119.516	147.090	155.551	165.581	177.273	

Monetary aggregates (end of period): *Money (M1)* includes demand deposits and currency outside banks. *Quasi money (QM)* include time, savings and foreign currency deposits. Eurostat has converted national currencies to the US dollar by applying the International Monetary Fund annual end of period exchange rates.

Total reserves (gold excluded, end of period): the statistics on official foreign reserves are extracted from the IMF's monthly *International Financial Statistics (IFS)*. Total reserves (gold excluded) are defined as the sum of central bank holdings of foreign currencies and other (gross) claims on non-residents; this definition excludes claims on residents denominated in foreign currency. According to the definition; official foreign reserves are calculated at market exchange rates and prices in force at the end of the period under consideration. Total reserves (gold excluded) published in *IFS* may differ from the figures published by the national authorities. Some factors contributing to possible differences are the valuation of the reserve position in the Fund, and a different treatment of claims in non-convertible currencies.

Average short term interest rates: data are extracted from the IMF's monthly *International Financial Statistics (IFS)*. Average short-term lending and deposit rates relate to period averages. *Lending rates* generally consist of the average interest rate charged on loans granted by reporting banks. *Deposit rates* relate to average demand and time deposit rates or average time deposit rates. These rates may not be strictly comparable across countries to the extent the representative value of the reporting banks and the weighting schemes vary.

USD exchange rates: international Monetary Fund exchange rates as present in the publication *Statistiques financières internationales*.

Inflation (twelve months changes)

Percentage change of the CPIs with the current month compared with the corresponding month of the previous year (t/t – 12).

	Jan.	Feb.	March	April	May	June	July	Aug.	Sept.	Oct.	Nov.	Dec.
1993												
1994	20.6	19.9	19.7	21.7	20.6	21.6	22.3	22.5	22.0	20.9	20.4	19.5
1995	19.7	19.5	18.2	15.2	15.2	14.0	12.6	11.4	10.8	9.4	8.9	8.9
1996	8.3	8.5	9.6	11.5	11.0	10.6	10.8	10.5	9.7	10.4	9.3	9.1

Inflation (% change of CPI)

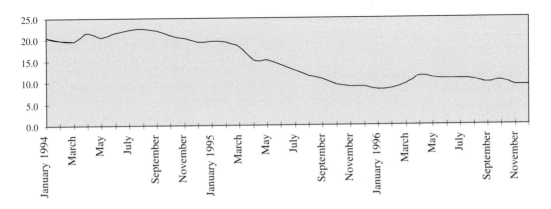

Inflation (twelve months changes): inflation rates (twelve months changes) are percentage changes of the CPIs with the current month compared with the corresponding month of the previous year. Inflation rates are based on national CPIs which are not strictly comparable between candidate countries or with those based on EU HICPs (different methods, concepts, practices in the calculation of CPIs). Inflation rates (twelve months changes) is based on ILO data.

Industry

Structure of GDP by economic activities (NACE, current prices)	1993	1994	1995	1996
	In % of Gross Domestic Product			
Mining and quarrying	1.2	1.3	1.2	
Manufacturing	29.5	29.7	28.1	
Production and distribution of electricity, gas and water	2.7	2.8	2.8	
Industrial production volume indices by NACE classes	Previous year = 100			
Total		106.4	102.0	101.0
Mining and quarrying		94.9	100.9	100.4
Manufacturing		106.7	102.6	101.1
Production and distribution of electricity, gas and water		107.8	99.7	100.8

Industrial production volume indices by NACE classes	1993 Q1	1993 Q2	1993 Q3	1993 Q4	1994 Q1	1994 Q2	1994 Q3	1994 Q4
	Corresponding period of the previous year = 100							
Total								
Mining and quarrying								
Manufacturing								
Production and distribution of electricity, gas and water								

	1995 Q1	1995 Q2	1995 Q3	1995 Q4	1996 Q1	1996 Q2	1996 Q3	1996 Q4
	Corresponding period of the previous year = 100							
	109.6	101.6	98.8	98.3	94.9	99.2	103.4	107.1
	104.5	97.7	109.8	93.4	86.0	103.5	119.5	94.6
	110.5	103.3	100.6	96.6	96.2	98.9	103.0	106.5
	107.7	84.1	115.1	95.5	99.3	99.0	91.5	112.0

Structure of GDP by economic activities (NACE, current prices): the structure of GDP by economic activities (NACE) is calculated *at market prices.*

Industrial production volume indices by NACE classes: industrial production covers mining and quarrying, manufacturing and electricity, gas and water supply (according to the NACE Classification Sections C, D, E). Index of Industrial Production covers enterprises with ten or more employees, except those engaged in the following activities: publishing, gas, steam and water supply.

Infrastructure

	1993	1994	1995
	In km per 1 000 km²		
Railway network			59
Railway transport	In million ton or passenger-km		
Freight transport			
Passenger transport	566	590	595
	In 1 000 of population		
Number of telephone subscribers			310
	Inhabitants		
Number of inhabitants per passenger car			2.8

Agriculture

	1992	1993	1994	1995	1996
Land area by land-use categories	In 1 000 hectares				
Total	2 025	2 025	2 025	2 025	2 025
Agricultural land	777	773	751	783	
Forest	1 071	1 071	1 094	1 098	
Arable land	245	245	234	230	230
Permanent meadows and pastures	560	558	501		417
Agricultural land by legal status	In % of agricultural land				
State enterprise					
Cooperatives					
Others					
Share of GDP	In % of Gross Domestic Product				
Agriculture, hunting, forestry and fishing (Nace A+B)		4.3	4.3		
	Previous year = 100				
Gross agricultural production volume indices		96.5	106.4	103.6	
Main crops by area	In 1 000 hectares				
Cereals	117.5	119.6	110.5	107	107.0
of which: wheat	42.6	43.7	42.0	42	40.8
Potatoes	30.0	29.0	23.0	24	22.0
Sugar beet	3.0	3.0	5.0	6	6.0
Fodder beet	6.0	6.0	6.0	6	4.0
Main crops by yield	In 100 kg/hectares				
Cereals	36.2	38.0	51.0	50.3	
of which: wheat	41.9	38.4	43.3	42.3	39.4
Potatoes	122.0	127.0	174.0	190.0	204.0
Sugar beet	306.0	379.0	452.0	432.0	485.0
Fodder beet	171.8	190.5	319.3	313.1	
Sales or procurement of animal for slaughter	In 1 000 tons of live weight				
Pigs			39.2	41.6	43.8
Cattle			30.8	35.2	37.8
Poultry			58.5	64.5	63.8
Livestock breeding intensity (end of period)	Heads per 1 000 ha of agricultural land				
Cattle			603	627	
of which: cows			262	268	
Sheep			23	35	
	Heads per 1 000 ha of arable land				
Pigs			2 440	2 530	
of which: sows					

Share of GDP: the structure of GDP by economic activities (NACE) is calculated *at market prices.*

Gross agricultural production volume indices: sliding average values of purchase prices in the last three years.

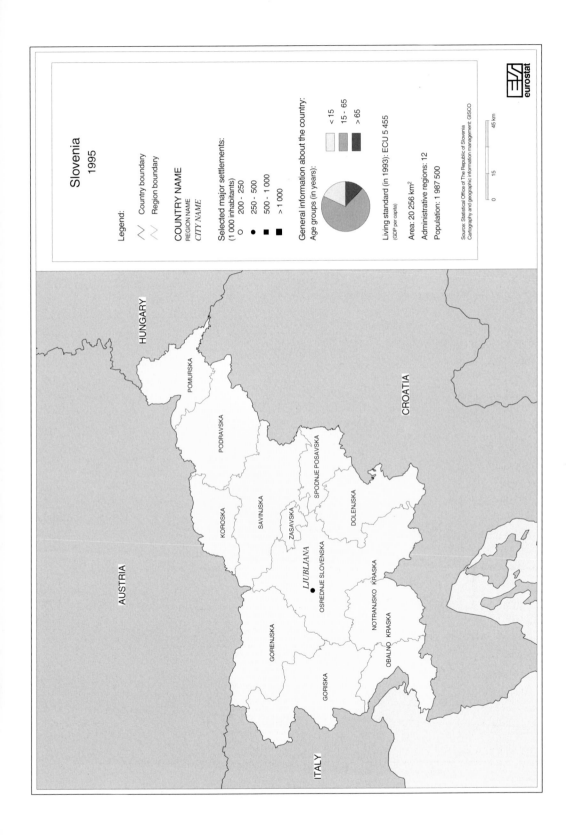

Slovenia
1995

Legend:

∧∧ Country boundary
∧∧ Region boundary

COUNTRY NAME
REGION NAME
CITY NAME

Selected major settlements:
(1 000 inhabitants)
○ 200 - 250
● 250 - 500
■ 500 - 1 000
■ > 1 000

General information about the country:

Age groups (in years):

□ < 15
▨ 15 - 65
■ > 65

Living standard (in 1993): ECU 5 455
(GDP per capita)

Area: 20 256 km²
Administrative regions: 12
Population: 1 987 500

Source: Statistical Office of The Republic of Slovenia
Cartography and geographic information management: GISCO

0   15   45 km

eurostat

HUNGARY

AUSTRIA

ITALY

CROATIA

POMURSKA

PODRAVSKA

KOROSKA

SAVINJSKA

ZASAVSKA

SPODNJE POSAVSKA

DOLENJSKA

GORENJSKA

LJUBLJANA
OSREDNJE SLOVENSKA

NOTRANJSKO KRASKA

OBALNO KRASKA

GORISKA

European Commission

Commission opinion on Slovenia's application for membership of the European Union

Supplement 15/97 to the Bulletin of the European Union

Luxembourg: Office for Official Publications of the European Communities

1997 — 103 pp. — 17.6 × 25.0 cm

ISBN 92-828-1237-5

Price (excluding VAT) in Luxembourg: ECU 7